RUNAWAYS

RUNAWAYS: THE COMPLETE COLLECTION VOL. 1. Contains material originally published in magazine form as RUNAWAYS #1-18. Fifth printing 2018. ISBN 978-0-7851-8558-1. Published by MARVEL WORLDWIDE, INC., a subsidiary of MARVEL ENTERTAINMENT, LLC. OFFICE OF PUBLICATION: 135 West 50th Street, New York, NY 10020. Copyright © 2014 MARVEL No similarity between any of the names, characters, persons, and/or institutions in this magazine with those of any living or dead person or institution is intended, and any such similarity which may exist is purely coincidental. **Printed in the U.S.A.** DAN BUCKLEY, President, Marvel Entertainment; JOHN NEE, Publisher; JOE QUESADA, Chief Creative Officer; TOM BREVOORT, SVP of Publishing; DAVID BOGART, SVP of Business Affairs & Operations, Publishing & Partnership; DAVID GABRIEL, SVP of Sales & Marketing, Publishing; JEFF YOUNGQUIST, VP of Production & Special Projects; DAN CARR, Executive Director of Publishing Technology; ALEX MORALES, Director of Publishing Operations; DAN EDINGTON, Managing Editor; SUSAN CRESPI, Production Manager; STAN LEE, Chairman Emeritus. For information regarding advertising in Marvel Comics or on Marvel.com, please contact Vit DeBellis, Custom Solutions & Integrated Advertising Manager, at vdebellis@marvel.com. For Marvel subscription inquiries, please call 888-511-5480. **Manufactured between 6/6/2018 and 6/26/2018 by QUAD GRAPHICS SARATOGA, SARATOGA SPRINGS, NY, USA.**

1 0 9 8 7 6 5

RUNAWAYS

WRITER: **BRIAN K. VAUGHAN**

PENCILS: **ADRIAN ALPHONA** (#1-10, #13-18) & **TAKESHI MIYAZAWA** (#11-12)

INKS: **DAVID NEWBOLD** (#1-5, #11-12) & **CRAIG YEUNG** (#6-10, #13-18)

COLORS: **BRIAN REBER** (#1-7, #11-12) & **CHRISTINA STRAIN** (#8-10, #13-18)

LETTERS: **PAUL TUTRONE** (#1), **CHRIS ELIOPOULOS** (#2-4, #10)
& **RANDY GENTILE** (#5-9, #11-18)

COVER ART: **JO CHEN** (#1-6, #8-10, #13-18), **ADRIAN ALPHONA** & **CRAIG YEUNG** (#7)
AND **JOSH MIDDLETON** (#11-12)

COLLECTION COVER: **ADRIAN ALPHONA** & **CHRISTINA STRAIN**

ASSISTANT EDITORS: **STEPHANIE MOORE** & **MACKENZIE CADENHEAD**

EDITOR: **C.B. CEBULSKI**

RUNAWAYS CREATED BY **BRIAN K. VAUGHAN** & **ADRIAN ALPHONA**

COLLECTION EDITOR: **JENNIFER GRÜNWALD**
ASSISTANT EDITOR: **CAITLIN O'CONNELL**
ASSOCIATE MANAGING EDITOR: **KATERI WOODY**
EDITOR, SPECIAL PROJECTS: **MARK D. BEAZLEY**
VP PRODUCTION & SPECIAL PROJECTS: **JEFF YOUNGQUIST**
SVP PRINT, SALES & MARKETING: **DAVID GABRIEL**

EDITOR IN CHIEF: **C.B. CEBULSKI**
CHIEF CREATIVE OFFICER: **JOE QUESADA**
PRESIDENT: **DAN BUCKLEY**
EXECUTIVE PRODUCER: **ALAN FINE**

INTROD

First of all, I don't hate my parents.

Yes, I did name Alex Wilder's evil mom and dad after my folks, but I swear that Catherine and Geoffrey Vaughan are delightful human beings who never beat me, threw away my comic collection and/or killed young girls in sacrificial rituals.

(My kid sister, Molly Hayes Vaughan, however, is just as adorable and powerful as her namesake.)

Still, I always thought that there was something slightly suspicious about the way adult comic writers had protagonists like Spider-Man and Batman revere their guardians. I mean, if Uncle Ben or Dr. and Mrs. Wayne had lived to see their children turn seventeen, Peter and Bruce probably would have ended up hating them, the way so many kids grow apart from their parents around that age. To me, it felt like grown-up comic creators were subtly suggesting to their young readers that true heroes always respect their elders and blindly follow their teachings.

(On the other hand, maybe the real message was that the only good parent is a dead one?)

Anyway, despite my severe lack of hair, I'm still a fairly young dude who thinks that it's always important to question authority and challenge the status quo established by the previous generation.

Thankfully, the decidedly non-evil adults at Marvel (including the always supportive Joe Quesada, Dan Buckley and Bill Jemas) were either too cool or too busy to stop me from turning my subversive agenda into an all-ages book filled with decoder rings, secret hideouts and everything I loved about comics as a kid.

If I'm the Runaways' mommy dearest, artist Adrian Alphona is definitely our kids' big daddy. Back when he was a relative newcomer to the medium, Adrian sent in a few sketches that immediately brought my two-dimensional character descriptions to life. Along with being a great storyteller, Adrian is also the undisputed king of fashion in comics. I defy you to find another "teen book" on the market where the teenagers look as true as they do in Adrian's panels. Even when he's drawing a telepathic dinosaur from the 87th century (whose facial expressions Adrian bases on his pet dog), my partner-in-crime always makes the fantastic feel absolutely real.

Obviously, Adrian and I couldn't have brought our baby into the world without a lot of help from countless collaborators, including powerhouse penciler Takeshi Miyazawa, incredible inkers David Newbold and Craig Yeung, courageous colorists Brian Reber and UDON's Christina Strain, laudable letterers like Virtual Calligraphy's Randy Gentile and David Sharpe, and especially ever-excellent editors C.B. Cebulski and MacKenzie Cadenhead. And we all owe a tremendous debt of gratitude to Stan "The Man" Lee, whose work at the House of Ideas helped inspire not only our book's classical high concept, but also my own off-putting obsession with alliteration.

In addition, I have to thank every kid who wasn't mean to me from kindergarten through senior year at NYU, since each of the Runaways is a composite of so many of you, my friends. And maximum respect to my brilliant wife Ruth McKee, who told me that the book should simply be called "Runaways" way back when I stupidly thought it should have a title like "SuperKrunk6" to appeal to the hipster kids of today.

UCTION

(Sorry, I may not be an adult yet, but I'm not cool either.)

Finally, I'd be remiss not to recognize the amazing work of one of the best artists in the medium, Ms. Jo Chen, who painted almost every cover of our initial run (with the exception of the Cloak and Dagger two-parter, which was handled by the equally sensational Joshua Middleton). I have it on good authority that it was the come-hither look Jo gave Nico on her unforgettable first cover that inspired Buffy the Vampire creator/my personal hero/dirty old man Joss Whedon to pick up our book, and he's been one of our most loyal backers ever since.

Speaking of our devoted readership, this series probably would have been cancelled three issues in if it weren't for the tireless support of people like you. I know I sound like a bad PBS pledge drive, but really, new books starring all-new characters are just not supposed to survive in today's crowded marketplace. The conventional wisdom is that comic fans only want to read about old characters, but Honorary Runaways like Mindy Owens (dedicated webmistress of www.runawaysthecomic.com) fought long and hard to help get our book into the hands of a whole new audience.

Not too long ago, we were all pretty sure that the eighteen issues you hold in your hands were going to be the last we'd ever see of the Runaways, but because of you, our heroes are back, and I look forward to writing their ongoing adventures until the day I die... or at least until the day I finally succumb to adulthood, at which point, I hope that one of you young writers reading this now will rightfully take my place.

For now, thank you all from the bottom of my Hostel for loving these characters as much as I do. Enjoy this special collection, and remember that under the bed is the first place evil parents usually check for contraband, so be sure to hide your copy in that special spot in your neighbor's backyard!

Keep running,
BKV

A Secret Location
2005

Daredevil, what's the sit-rep?

If we don't find a way to put the Hulk down fast, he's gonna tear right through the *White House!*

It's Spider-Man, Cap, he's... he's *dead!*

Don't worry, gentlemen, *I* can handle this!

After all, there's more than one way to soothe a savage beast.

Okay, wait. Time out for a second.

This is totally retarded.

We're able to afford a home here, *young man*, because *my* father taught me that *every* dollar makes a difference.

Then let me get a job! Please! I could--

Cancel the service. *Today.*

Yes, sir.

I know you think I'm a monster, Alex, but someday you'll understand that everything I did was done out of love.

And when that day comes... I hope you remember to put your mother and me in a decent *nursing home.*

For now, I would appreciate it if you'd simply change into something *clean.*

Our guests will be here at seven.

Jeez, he's in a mood.

I'm sorry, honey, but you know how nervous he gets before these things.

I don't understand *why*. Every year, you guys just invite the same five couples over to sip brandy and cut checks.

When other people in L.A. do charity events, they put on, you know, celebrity golf tournaments... fun stuff.

Alex, your father and I have told you, good deeds should be done in *secret*, with no expectation of reward. It's what makes us human.

Yeah, I know. I just wish I didn't have to babysit your friends' creepy kids while you guys get to hide in the library.

We're not *hiding*. We're doing sensitive work in private. And those five children are anything but "creepy".

Oh, yeah? What about that white guy who always calls me "brother"? Or that dorky girl who still hasn't given me back the *Prisoner* DVDs I let her borrow *last* year?

Alex, you're being obnoxious. The six of you have been having nothing but marvelous times together since you were all in diapers.

And unlike your "internet friends", those kids think of you as *family*. They can't *wait* to see you!

The Hayes Residence
6:37 P.M.

Alex, get down here, please!

We have *company!*

Al-*ex!* What's happenin', brother?

Hello, *Chase.*

Sorry we're late, all! Big pile-up on Cliffside.

Alex, you remember our daughter *Nico*, don't you?

Holy...

The Game Room
8:46 P.M.

≈Yawn≈

What she said.

Listen, I know we'd all rather be somewhere else right now, but we're stuck here for at least another hour, so we might as well *try* to amuse ourselves.

So what's the plan, man?

Please be beer, please be beer, please be beer...

Hee.

Let's spy on the 'rents.

Alex, is... is everything all right up here?

Uh, yeah, totally. We were just fooling around with one of *your* old games.

And you think *Vice City* is dirty.

Why? Is everything all right with *you*?

Of course. It's just, we heard yelling, and we were afraid...

Well, I'm glad you're all *okay*.

Anyway, your parents and I are almost done with the last draft of the new fundraising charter. We'll be up in a few.

Try not to break anything *expensive* before then?

Heh, not a problem, Mrs. W.

PAYCE

SLAM

≥whew≤

I have never run... so fast... in *my life*.

Do you think she bought it, Alex?

I don't know. I... I think I'm gonna puke.

PAYCE

Okay, will someone *please* tell me what's going on? What did I miss down there?

Why'd we stop Twistering? We just started!

Gert, take Molly to the bathroom or something.

Why?

So we can fill Karolina in on what happened, okay?

But this involves *Molly's* parents, too! She deserves to know the truth!

She's just a kid!

She's old enough to know her parents are *evil!*

Um, *helloooo.* I *know* what you guys are whispering about...

You... you do?

Duh.

S... E... X. I'm not a *baby*.

Fine.

Come on, kid. Let's go powder our noses.

That's code for *pee*, right?

What the heck is going on, guys? You're scaring me.

Karolina, you... you better sit down. I don't know how to tell you this, but--

Alex's dad just killed some chick.

No! *God,* please, I swear I'm not lying!

Listen, even *if* you're telling the truth--which seventeen years on the job tells me you're clearly *not*-- meta-crime isn't our jurisdiction.

Try the super-freaks in Manhattan. I think the Avengers got some kinda hotline.

No kidding. I've been calling it since I was *eight!* It's just a machine! And they don't respond to anything unless it's, like, a full-scale alien invasion!

Besides, by the time Captain America checks his voicemail, our parents will probably have butchered a *dozen* other--

KLICK

Told you.

Guess we're on our own.

We can't just give up! The police will *have* to believe us if we bring them some kinda evidence.

Like what, one of our parents' Halloween masks?

No, more like a *body*.

Exactly. Where's the trunk now?

Trunk? *What* trunk?

Why does it always feel like I accidentally skipped a chapter?

Gert's dad probably already dumped it into the *tar pits* or something, Nico.

Actually, he and my mom carried it inside as soon as we got home.

And you think it's still there? With the... the *girl* in it?

One way to find out.

Hey, here's one of those security keypad things.

Don't touch it! You'll probably set off sirens and stuff!

Looks like we need a five-digit password, something with the numbers three, four and seven.

How can you tell?

Those keys are a *smidge* darker than the other ones, from the oil on your fingertips, you know?

Get out! That is so *C.S.I.*, Nico!

Are there letters with the numbers?

Yeah, like on a phone. Why? What can you spell with those three digits?

Pride.

What the %@#*?!

Nobody move! They... they can only sense motion.

What do you mean "they"? What is it?!

That thing from *Jurassic Park*. A... A *Velociraptor*.

That's impossible, Alex! They're not--

Ahh, get it away!

Chill, Karolina. It's gotta be C.G.I. or whatever. I'll prove it.

Chase...

Don't!

Put it down!

You're gonna get us *killed!*

Mom?

Dad?

Everybody, run! I'll try to hold them--

--off?

Wait, the dinosaur is real, but her *parents* are C.G.I.?

No, I... I think those are *holograms*.

Hey, squirt. I'm sorry, but if you're watching this projection we recorded... your mother and I are probably *dead.*

What?

Is this a joke? It's written in some *foreign* language.

It may seem like gibberish now, but it will all make perfect sense once you've deciphered the text.

Just use the decoder ring Mr. Dean gave you when you turned eighteen.

My parents gave you a *ring*?

No, and I'm only *fifteen*! I don't know *what* they're talking about!

You may need help with this adjustment period, so seek out whichever members of The Pride are still alive. *They're* your family now.

You've always known the world was being run into the ground by a bunch of brainless cowards, but the future belongs to great minds like *you*...

...so *steal* tomorrow from them and make it your *own*.

Okay, um... *huh*?

So can we go to the police now? *Please*?

With what? We've got Gert's parents claiming they're some kind of *time travelers*, but we still don't have any evidence that they helped kill that *girl*.

Are you *nuts*? They've got *psychic raptors* in their basement!

And Siegfried and Roy have **white tigers** in theirs. Doesn't mean they're criminals, just means they're... **odd.**

Gert's right. This definitely proves we're onto something huge, but we still need a smoking gun to put our parents away for good.

Without it, they'll probably just Shapiro their way out of jail and kill us as soon as they're free.

What about that not-so-little black book of theirs? Didn't they say it's got info on all of their crimes and stuff? Maybe it says where they hid the girl's body.

And all we have to do is decipher the thing, right? So let's go to Karolina's house and look for that magic decrypto ring.

My house? But... but my parents can't **really** be part of this. They might be a little eccentric, but they're not **evil.** They don't even eat **meat!**

Well, neither did **Hitler.**

Karolina, if you'd seen what the rest of us saw back at my house, you'd understand. I'm with Nico. We should press on to your pad next.

But first, we have to figure out what to do with this... thing. Gert's parents said it's supposed to protect her, but they're not exactly **trustworthy.** Besides, the five of us are conspicuous enough as is.

Sorry, girl. Guess that means it's back in the doghouse for you. But don't worry, once this is all over, I promise to come back for you, okay?

I thought my life was weird **yesterday...**

This room's clean.

Any luck up there, Karolina?

Nope, and Nico and I have been through every jewelry box and trinket drawer in the house.

No offense, but I seriously don't think my parents are like the rest of yours. They're *good people.*

Although her mom does have more shoes than an entire season of *Cribs...*

Well, keep looking for some kind of switch or keypad thing. There's gotta be a trapdoor around here somewhere.

Why? Just because our houses were tricked out doesn't mean *this* place is.

Never fear, kiddies. Chase is on the case... and he just hit paydirt.

The Wilder Residence
4:21 A.M.

BRRING

Do you have *any idea* what time it is?

It's four in the morning, Mr. Wilder.

"Do you know where your children are?"

Lieutenant Flores?

Sorry to bother you, sire... but I think we might have a *problem.*

It's almost enough to make me forget I'm some kind of extraterrestrial *freak.*

Um, speaking of which, it's probably time for you to come back down to *earth.*

You want me to wear this *thing* again? But it... it represents everything my parents ever *lied* to me about.

Maybe, but that bracelet also turns off your *lightshow.* And right now, we can't have you floating around like an oversized Tinkerbell.

What do you mean *oversized?*

We need to stay below our parents' radar, Karolina. If you can do all this after a few minutes of practice, think what your *mom* and *dad* can do.

This whole super-villain club of theirs is turning out to be a lot more dangerous than any of us first thought.

Exactly, which is why I think our next move should be to get *Molly.*

I know you wanted to protect her from all this because she's just a little kid, but she's probably safer with *us* than she is in her *house.*

I mean, Molly's folks are part of this psycho Pride thing, too, right?

Gert's got a point, Alex.

Besides, if we keep the truth from Molly, how are we any better than our *parents?*

You are grounded until graduation.

At *least.*

That goes for you, too, Nico.

Mom? Dad? What... what are you doing here?

That's exactly what I was about to ask. Alex's mother called us in a panic to see if he was at *our* house. That's when we found out *you* were gone, too.

Your father and I have been scouring all of Los Angeles for you kids. What are you doing in Mr. Stein's workshop? Are... are you making *ecstasy*?

Nevermind. This is a conversation for tomorrow morning.

Right now, you're all going *home.*

Or what, Pop? You'll use some of your scary *toys* on us?

The Staff of One. Her... her body is *absorbing* it.

How...?

What is *wrong* with you, Mom? Snap *out* of it!

SNAP OUT OF IT!

Nico, no!

That's *enough*, young lady!

I'll discipline my *own* child, Victor! You take care of the Yorkes' girl!

helpme helpmehelpme helpme

Help yourself, Gertrude. By coming with *us*.

We have no intention of hurting *any* of you, we just want--

Sssssss

Hm?

RRAAAARRR

AHHHH!

GET IT OFF!

I *knew* you were out there.

Die, animal!

"VishNin rrK..."

SKREEECH

Sorry! Stupid manual transmission is *impossible!*

Where am I going, anyway?

The hospital! I've still got a... a giant *rod* stuck inside my body!

Heh.

Chase? You're *okay...?*

Uhn. Not really. Feels like I finished an entire keg by myself... and then dropped it on my *head*. And why am I wearing these stupid--

Ssssssss

Do you honestly think they'll fall for a *bluff* like that?

Well, if Wilder is right, they've already seen us slay one young girl.

I still can't believe they actually witnessed the *sacrifice.*

Can you imagine what must be going through their minds?

We would've had to tell them about The Pride when they turned eighteen anyway, love. All this does is advance our timetable slightly.

You sure your daughter isn't going to wake up in the middle of this, Doc?

Molly's being telepathically sedated. It's usually pretty effective.

God, I wish *we'd* had mutant powers when *Gertrude* was a baby. If you knew how many sleepless nights she--

Dale, put the samurai battle-axe away, will you? You know how weapons from alternate pasts make me *nervous.*

We need to be ready for anything, dear. These children are young, but that doesn't mean they're--

Mom...?

Mommy...?

Dammit, she's slipping out of the trance.

Everyone get out. *I'll* handle this.

I'm right here, Molly. You were talking in your sleep.

Bad dream?

My... my stomach is all hurtie.

Aw, do you want me to get you some 7-Up?

Nuh-uh. I've just been feeling *gross* all day, and... and everyone acts weird when I try to talk about it. Gert took me to the bathroom at Alex's house, and... and she said it sounded like I got a *curse* or something.

I didn't really believe her, but then a little blood came out of my--

Um, why don't you just try to go back to sleep, precious?

I know this can be a scary time in a young woman's life...

...but right now, Mommy has *other* things to worry about.

The Hayes' Residence
5:48 A.M.

I took the shuttlecraft back from New York as soon as I heard.

What about Frank, Leslie?

He's stuck in Manhattan, brokering some deal with another intergalactic arms trader. A Skrull, I think... they all look the same to me.

Where are the others?

My wife's upstairs with Molly, and the Wilders are preparing a contingency plan in case the children fail to show.

But the Steins and the Minorus aren't answering their communicators. We're worried that your daughter and the other kids might have *attacked* them.

Please, Karolina doesn't have the *spine* for a fight.

And God help any child who's stupid enough to make a move against *us*.

How about you, Delta Team?

You in position, over?

Dude, you're killing the battery on my two-way. For the billionth time, we're all in position and we all remember the plan.

Can we knock off your lame role-playing stuff and *do* this already?

Ah, roger that, this is Alpha Team, uh... proceeding with Phase One.

We won't all live through this, will we, Alex?

What are you talking about? We're going to be *fine*, Nico. We just have to stick to the--

People always say teenagers think they're immortal, but I... I don't think that. I mean, all I *ever* think about is death.

When my mom jammed that staff-thing into my chest, all I could think was... I'm surprised I even lived *this* long.

I know exactly what you mean.

You *do?*

Totally. Even *before* all this. It's like, every day, the people in charge seem to make the world a little more screwed-up, and we can see it, but there's nothing anyone our age can--

AHHHHH!

You guys all right?

Yeah, just make sure your pet keeps the good doctor here occupied.

Nico, you search upstairs, I'll take the--

KRAK!

ALEX!

Girls, I'm *disappointed.*

Call me old-fashioned, but all of this fighting seems very *unladylike.*

No!

AHN!

What did you *do?*

It... it was *instinct!* I didn't mean--

WHEN BLOOD IS SHED... LET THE STAFF OF ONE EMERGE--

UHN!

Where... where did you get your mother's--

FREEZE.

Nico? Are... are you *okay?* What did you do to my--

Keep an eye on these people, Gert. And when Alex comes to...

...tell him I'm on to Phase Three.

Let's go, Karolina! Take off your bracelet and let's storm the castle already!

Chase, we're supposed to wait for Alex to signal us with which room Molly's in before we make our move.

Oh, *dude...* I just remembered! These goggles I stole from my dad have some kinda *X-ray vision* in 'em!

Maybe I can use them to look *through* the walls and--

Something tells me this one isn't the *brains* of your operation.

AHHHH!

Hello, my angel.

MOM?!

Stop it! You're... you're hurting him!

Merely detaining him. You'll understand when you learn to use *your* beautiful gifts, Karolina. I'm just sorry you had to discover them like *this*.

Your father and I had always hoped to take you to our homeworld before we told you about your unique heritage.

So I... I really *am* an alien? You and Daddy *lied* to me?

No, Karolina, we *protected* you. We gave you what no other girl in Hollywood had... a *normal childhood*.

And please don't bother taking off that bracelet. You and I have the exact same abilities, and we can't use them to *hurt* each other.

You made me wear this *anchor* my entire life! And if your powers are the same as mine, then... then touching it must do the same thing to *you* that it does to *me*.

It must take away everything that makes you *special*.

Whoa.

Be cool, Mol. We're not going to hurt you.

You have a *dinosaur!*

Yeah, but she's a friendly dinosaur... like Barney.

I *hate* Barney!

Oh... well, uh, the confusing things you're feeling right now aren't *bad,* Molly. You're actually something called a *mutant,* a person born with--

No *duh,* Gert! I'm not confused about *that.* I'm confused about why Nico hit my mom in the *face!*

She *had* to, Molly. Your mom and dad might not seem like bad people... but they *are.*

You're not going to like what I'm about to say, but I hated when older kids tried to sugarcoat stuff with me, so I'm just going to tell it to you straight, okay?

Your parents-- *all* of our parents-- they're actually *super-villains,* like the bad guys you see on TV.

During that "costume party" we wouldn't let you watch, they *killed* an innocent kid... a girl who wasn't much older than you.

You're *lying!*

Just be *nice!*

Uhf!

FWOOM

What the *Hulk*?! Did you see how *strong* she is?

Wow. Thanks, Mol.

Man... that made me... *sleepy*...

Come on, time to move.

Wait, my mom's in the bottom of that *pool*! She's gonna *drown*!

Your mom's a *murderer*, Karolina.

She's my *mom*!

All right. I'll fish her out. I'm coming with you, Nico. The rest of you get to the van and have the motor running. If we're not out in three minutes... leave *without* us.

So your mom's staff just... came out from *inside* of you?

Yeah, right after Gert's dad *cut* me.

I don't know how to describe it. It's almost like my... my *soul* puked it up. Thing seems to work *me* more than I work *it*.

I'm just glad you're alive.

I know this probably isn't the right time to talk about it, but when we... when we *kissed*, it was like this little island of *all right* in an ocean of horrible--

This *isn't* the right time.

I agree, Alex.

Here we go.

You think she's still alive?

I'm not doing mouth-to-mouth if she's not.

Uhn!

Oh, my God.

Check it out...

Remember how Mr. Yorkes said that Karolina's parents had some kind of *decoder ring,* the one that supposedly deciphers their Playbook of Evil?

What if *this* is the ring he was--

VERMIN!

You think you've **beaten** us? We haven't even used a **fraction** of our strength against you.

Once the kid gloves come off, your parents will **annihilate** you. We brought you children into this world...

...and **we** can take you out.

KRAK!

Nice.

Speak softly, etc., etc.

Alex, what I said before, I didn't mean--

No, you were right, Nico.

We have more **important** things to worry about...

Damn, Mrs. Dean's ring only seems to be decoding *every other word* of this Abstract thing. I just hope there's enough dirt in here to put our parents away for good.

You sure you know the way to the police station, Karolina?

Yeah, I got arrested a few years ago when my parents took me to a *peace rally*.

I still can't believe that was all just an *act*. And I can't believe I *fell* for it.

Don't be so hard on yourself, gorgeous. Didn't your mom and dad both win *Emmys*? It's like, lying about who they really are is what your parents are *best* at.

What are we *doing*? I have to go to *school*!

It's okay, Molly. We're just going on a little field trip.

But my... my parents didn't sign a *permission slip*.

And they're never going to sign one again, Mol. The sooner you accept that, the sooner you'll--

DEET-DR-DEET-DEET

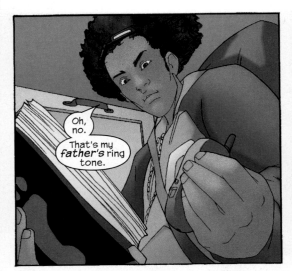

Oh, no.

That's my *father's* ring tone.

Hello?

Well, young man, I would say that this little misadventure violates the *curfew* we agreed upon, wouldn't you?

Save it, Dad. We're on our way to the cops now.

Really? Why don't you turn to AM 1070 in... five... four... three...

Police are still searching for sixteen-year-old **Alex Wilder**, wanted in connection with yesterday's murder in Malibu.

What?

Alex, look!

ELECTRIC LOUIE

Runaway **Destiny Gonzales** was found stabbed to death in the area teenager's bedroom late last night.

Police suspect that the brutal slaying may have been related to the young man's involvement in violent online role-playing games.

That's the girl *you* killed!

Quiet, son. You'll miss the best part.

Authorities are reportedly also looking for other local teens who may have **helped** commit this crime.

In addition, the Amber Alert system has been activated for eleven-year-old Molly Hayes, who was allegedly **kidnapped** by this gang just a few hours ago.

Nice try, Dad. But we'll **prove** that you framed us.

Prove? To **whom?** The **police?** Who do you think tipped us off that you had run away in the first place? The **media?** Who do you think I ordered to release this story?

Alex, my boy, this entire **city** belongs to The Pride.

But that doesn't mean we're *despots.* We're just concerned citizens who've made great sacrifices to make the world a better place for *you.*

And if you come home now, I swear that your mother and I will make all of your problems disappear.

I'd rather blow my own brains out than go back to your *lies.*

Listen to me, you little son of a--

Son of a *what,* Dad? What *exactly* am I the son of?

Alex, honey, it's your mother. Don't do this. *Please.* The Pride... these men and women, they will hunt you down and gut you like a--

≑klick≑

Well, *that* didn't sound too good.

We're dead. Our parents, they... they control *everything.* We're fugitives from the entire world.

Then there's only one thing left to do.

What's that?

Fall off the face of the earth.

Molly, they... they have *Molly*...

We know, love. But don't fear, Mr. and Mrs. Wilder have already put the back-up plan into effect.

The Minoru girl actually *struck* me.

Big deal, she froze *me* like a... a mystical *popsicle*.

How could they all *betray* us like this?

I'm not so sure that *all* of them have.

Molly, get off of Gert's dinosaur!

You're gonna hurt yourself!

And stop using the word "freaking" so much. It's freaking me out.

Arsenic says I can use any words I want to now, Alex. She says I don't have to do anything my *Mom and Dad* told me to do ever again.

First of all, her name is *Gertrude*, not "Arsenic". And secondly--

Gertrude is my *slave name*, Alex.

You can keep calling yourself whatever your evil parents named you, but the rest of us are *starting over*.

Right, Bruiser?

Right, Arsenic.

Aren't codenames supposed to be *cooler* than your actual names?

How's the code-breaking going, brother?

Slowly but surely.

I translated some of the first chapter, but I think it's mostly historical stuff. Whoever wrote this thing keeps talking about these weird six-toed giants called *Gibborim.*

Yeah, I'm pretty sure I've heard that word before, but I'd need a good search engine to confirm it.

Guess we're S.O.L. without D.S.L.

How about you, Chase? You and Karolina hide our wheels somewhere?

Yep, in *plain sight.*

I stole the plates off a Honda Civic and switched them with the ones on my van. It'll be months before that dude notices he's got the wrong license on his car.

Wait. *What?*

I warned you, send him to sell our cow and he'll come back with *magic beans...*

Listen, our parents' stormtroopers are looking for a white van with our plates, right? But now, if the cops see our ride and run the license, it'll come back totally clean, no red flags or nothing.

Trust me, I read it in this true crime book. Works every time.

Speaking of *dim bulbs*, did Lucy in the Sky just drop a few watts?

Oh, you mean my glow?

Yeah, Talkback noticed that I lose some of my intensity at night.

I figure blondie here gets her alien powers from the *sun*, like a solar-powered calculator, but bigger... and worse with numbers.

Hey, who are you calling *bigger*, Mr. Hand?

Sexual tension.

Gross.

That reminds me, has anyone seen--

My staff!

My staff is... is **gone**.

That creepy magic wand of yours?

You probably just misplaced it, Nic-- er, **Sister Grimm.** Took me about an hour to find my **off-switch** bracelet this morning.

There must be a million rooms in this funhouse.

Alex, it feels like I have something in my eye, but instead of my eye, it's... it's my **soul** or my--

I don't want to scare you, Nico, but when your mom stabbed you with that thing, it sorta disappeared into your **chest,** right?

Is there any chance when you went to sleep, your body, you know... **reabsorbed** it, or--

Can you guys make out later, please?

I'm freaking **starving.**

Food can wait, Molly. We haven't even figured out our next move against The Pride, and now Nico has something *inside* of her.

Well, at least *one* of us does. I'm with Bruiser. We haven't eaten in, like, twelve hours.

Maybe he's right, Alex. I'm... I'm probably just hungry.

Either way, what are we supposed to do? Call *Domino's*?

We can't use our credit cards or make ATM withdrawals without alerting the entire world to our whereabouts, and we only have nineteen bucks between us in cash.

Dude, your parents' fancy-pants lifestyle has made you *soft*. Nineteen bucks is enough to buy six people a *feast* at the local Circle A.

Fine. But if we're leaving the Hostel, we're going as a *group*. I don't want you coming back with any more magic beans.

Magic *what?*

Gert, stay here and keep an eye on Molly, will you?

Hey, why do I have to stay? I'm a *mutant*, 'member? I'm stronger than all you guys combined!

Don't worry, kid, if they forget to bring back Slim Jims for us, Old Lace here will teach them a lesson about the *food chain.*

RRRRRR

I don't know, Alex. These "disguises" make us look like those politically correct, multi-ethnic gangs that only rob people in bad TV shows.

Um, speaking of *robberies*...

Ah, crap.

Yep!

No.

Sort of.

If we don't get out of here fast, we're gonna be super-*incarcerated.*

Right. Let's grab some grub and scramble.

You're welcome to come with us, uh...?

Oh. *Topher.*

My name is Topher.

Hey, who said this punk could come back to *my* hideout?

It's not *your* hideout, it's *our* base. Besides, Chase, if we turn our backs on this kid, how are *we* any better than our--

Whoa, don't use my real name around this dude!

Talkback, be *nice.*

Why should I? This freak and his two pals just tried to knock over the Circle A! At *gunpoint!* We should leave him for the pigs!

No, please! I told you, those were my *parents!* They *made* me come with them! They're... they're *evil!*

Sound familiar?

That's *his* story. Why should we believe him?

Look into his *eyes*, Talkback. He's obviously been through the same stuff we have.

Five-oh! Everybody, West Wing!

WOoooWOoooWOooOO

"West Wing?"

Walk fast, talk fast.

You have to learn to speak *"Alex"* if you're gonna run with the Children of the Damned...

Hold on. All of *your* parents are evil, too?

Lucy in the Sky, give him the Cliffs Notes.

Six of us ran away from home after we found out that our parents are part of this sick secret society called The Pride... and I mean *bad* sick, not cool sick.

They framed us for a murder we didn't commit, but we're using the powers and weapons we took from them to try and *help* people.

Wow, you're... you're like a junior version of the A-Team.

What's an A-Team?

Sorry, guess my interests are a little more... *retro* than yours.

How *old* are you guys, anyway?

Well, *Bruiser* is our youngest. She's eleven. She's back at The Hostel with Arsenic, who's fourteen or fifteen, I think.

Alex, Sister Grimm and I are all sixteen.

Oh, same here.

Believe it or not, Talkback up there is the elder statesman of our crew.

Yeah, I remember sixteen...

WOOOOWOOOWOOOO

...back when life was *simple.*

Nico, we've got two black-and-whites on our six.

Think you can take 'em?

I'll give it a shot, Alex.

Or I'll *get* shot...

{SMOKE}

SKREEEE KERASSSH

Huh, wonder why I didn't accidentally conjure up a bunch of birds *that* time? Maybe I can't cast the same spell *twice*?

How...?

She's pretty hardcore, huh? Sister Grimm is actually the daughter of two *sorcerers.*

What kind of bad guys are *your* parents, Topher? Androids? Demons? *Android demons?*

Um, none of the above, really. See, they both work-- *worked*-- for this power company in Sacramento.

There was some kinda accident at the plant, and when they got caught in the blast, they turned super-fast and super-strong, but also, you know... totally *nuts.*

They got fired 'cause they were too unstable to work, so they started robbing stores for cash.

Jeez, didn't they get workers' comp or anything?

I... I don't know. They just said they'd *kill* me if I didn't help them. And now they're out there somewhere, sick and confused, and... and I don't know what to--

Don't worry, Toph. You can crash at our place until the heat dies down, and I'll help you find your mom and dad first thing tomorrow morning.

It's like they teach you in first grade, if you ever lose your parents in a public place, just stay calm...

...they're bound to turn up soon.

Would you like a snack, Geoffrey?

I came down to fix myself some warm milk, and noticed that the neighbors had left a *bundt cake* on our porch.

"We were so sorry to hear about Alex on the news, but everyone in the neighborhood knows that your son is innocent, and you are all in our prayers."

Prayers. Lord, I sometimes forget what a pack of *imbeciles* we're surrounded by.

Well, I just got a late-night gift of my own.

The Pride's operative in Robbery/Homicide e-mailed me a few minutes of surveillance footage taken earlier tonight.

Really? What is it?

An answer to our prayers.

That's Alex! Where... where was this taken?

A convenience store in Los Feliz.

The kids are still in *California*? I thought they'd be halfway to *Canada* by now!

Do we know who they're fighting here?

A trio of thieves... new players. Whoever they are, they certainly didn't request a permit from The Pride to rob stores in *our* city.

Regardless, if the children have opted to start playing crimefighter, it's more imperative than ever that we find them quickly...

...before some two-bit hood makes an *example* out of them.

Home again, home again...

WHOA! This place is the--

RARRRRARR

AHHH! WHAT IS IT?!

Oh, my God!

Where's Arsenic?!

HELP ME!

I'm here! I'm here!

Gert, call off your raptor!

I'm trying! Old Lace... she's not listening to my thoughts!

Then think harder, Arse! She's, uhh, too heavy to budge!

Says you, wimpster...

Scooch.

Old Lace, play *nice!*

See, she wasn't trying to hurt anybody. She just likes roughhousing.

Isn't that right, you big silly-head?

RRRRRRR

So, you guys bring back burritos?

Ah, you can eat *mine*, Molly.

You... you have a *dinosaur*!

And you have an earring in your eyebrow.

Are you in a band?

What... what *are* you?

I'm a mutant but not a bad one like Magneto a good one like Doop and the X-Statix and when I grow up I'm gonna join the X-Men and get married to Wolverine so you better not act prejudiced around me.

'Kay?

Of course not. Some of my best friends are mutants.

For serious?

Oh, brother...

Topher, this is *Gert*, whose manners are only slightly better than her *pet's*.

My *name* is... never mind.

Tell me, Never Mind, does that thing always try to eat guests?

Dunno. You're our first.

Topher is one of us, Arsenic. His parents are *eeeevil*.

If that's our only criteria for admission, this cave is gonna fill up *fast*.

Come on, Topher, I'll give you the nickel tour of the joint.

Yeah, I think I'll join you.

That's okay, Alex.

I've got it.

Told you this was a bad idea, bro...

Hey, can you guys do me a favor?

If Topher asks about my *powers* or whatever, could you please not mention that I'm, you know...?

An alien?

Shh! I don't want to make him any more freaked out than he already is, okay?

Topher doesn't need to know I'm not... not from this *planet.* If he says anything, just tell him I'm a *mutant.*

Why? You know we'd accept you even if you were from *France,* Karolina! You shouldn't be--

God, I'm just asking you to do *one thing,* Chase!

You don't have to be such a...

Forget it, it's late.

I'm going to bed.

Man, this is just like the Real World... only *real.*

I'm sorry, did I--

No, it's just, there's kind of *someone else.* I don't think we're exclusive or anything yet, but we... we *kissed,* right after all of this started happening.

You and Talkback?

Eww, no!

Alex.

Really? I mean, he seems like a great guy... but not exactly the kind of boy I picture being your *type.*

He's not. Not exactly. But we've both been through the same unbelievable experience, like two people who survived a plane crash together or something, right?

There aren't a lot of guys out there who understand what it's like to discover that the people who got you a *clown* for your seventh birthday are actually *super-villains.*

Well, for what it's worth... there's one more now.

Thanks, Topher. But I'm afraid I... I still can't kiss you.

Don't be afraid, Nico.

Everything okay up here?

Alex?

Yeah, uh, everything is--

Actually, I was just about to leave.

Topher, wait!

I should really get some shut-eye, Nico. My parents have had me on the run ever since their accident, and--

Fine, you can take a room in the *east* wing.

Nico, you and I need to *talk*.

DANGER
GAMMA
TESTING SITE
LETHAL LEVELS OF
RADIATION!

I don't know what to say, Alex. You've been so sweet to me, and I've been acting like a total--

Nico...

No, you have to hear this. I just did something completely awful, and you deserve to--

Nico, I already know that you and Topher kissed.

You... you do?

HOW?

Oh, our first night in the Hostel, I found this *secret room* next door. It's sorta like those passageways in my parents'--

You've been *spying* on me?

HNNNNK... SHOOOOOOO...

CHUH... ZZZZNNN...

Kill me.

Gert!

My *name* is--

Have you seen Nico?

You mean Sister Grimm?

Enough with the stupid names already!

When are you going to *grow up*?

Sorry, Peter Pan.

I thought not growing up was the whole *point* of this little club.

Never mind.

I'll find her *myself*...

GWUHHH!

What is *wrong* with you?

Me?! You're the one kissing *my* guy!

Your guy? What about Alex?

How many guys do you *have*?

Get off, *jerk!*

I'm not the jerk, *you're* the--

RAAAAAAR

Hey, that's not--

I don't know how you sucked all the girl power out of this place so fast, sport, but maybe you should just--

Ahn!

AHHHHHH!

Nico! What's *happening?*

Just give her some room, Karolina.

Everything's going to be all right now.

‹nnn‹

Nico and I figured out that her body **reabsorbs** her staff after every couple of uses. Just let her catch her breath and--

Get... get away from me.

But--

I... I have to get out of this place.

Nico, hold up!

Yeah, wait for--

Alex, maybe you should give her some space.

But I... I...

Carry a torch for her? Noted.

But it's like they say, if you love something...

"...set it free."

Any progress, dear?

Some.

The rest of The Pride and I have been attempting to identify the three unregistered rogues who attacked our children.

So far, all we know is that at least two of the trio appear to possess augmented strength, speed, and some degree of invulnerability.

Well then, they're most likely *mutants*, no?

That's precisely what I was about to ask the good Dr. Hayes.

It's possible, Wilder, but not likely.

My pureblood union notwithstanding, it's extremely rare to encounter more than one mutant with the exact same power.

These lowlifes probably just stumbled onto a cursed artifact or... or *radioactive meteorite.* You know, the usual.

What say you, Leslie?

You mean, do I think *extra-terrestrials* robbed that convenience store?

If so, my lot has started setting its sights considerably lower.

Hhhmm. Any luck on your end, Victor?

Perhaps. My nulloscope found a latent print on one of the weapons recovered at the crime scene.

I ran it past your boy in the LAPD, and he says the fingerprint belongs to some drifter who got pinched just once... in 1939.

Impossible.

Unless... could these be *your* people, Yorkes?

I sincerely doubt it, Geoffrey. As far as I know, Dale and I are the only time travelers to have pierced the fourth dimension within the last temporal phase.

Mr. Wilder, this is the Minoru clan chiming in. We're going to suggest another possibility...

...but we don't think you're going to *like* it.

Nico? Where **are** you?

Come on, your friends say it's not **safe** to be out here!

≷sniff≷

They're not my friends. They're just a bunch of kids stuck in the same sinking ship as me.

Well, **I'm** your friend, okay?

I'm so sorry, Topher.

First, you... you had to deal with your sick parents, and now, you have to put up with us bickering little **spazzes.**

Hey, you want to know a secret?

Those two people I was with at the Circle A... they weren't **really** my parents, and they **didn't** get their powers from some "industrial accident".

I... I don't understand. Where **did** they get their powers from?

You see, I'm not really sixteen years old.

I was born at the turn of the century.

You're *four*?

Huh?

Oh, no, *last* century. In 1900.

Eww! And I *kissed* you?

Cute.

Yeah, I got turned when I was your age. Made a small fortune in stocks after the Depression, then lost it all after the dot-com crash.

Holding up all-night liquor joints is a drag, but I've grown accustomed to a rather *expensive* lifestyle over the decades, you know?

So all that stuff you told us...

...was a *lie*? Yeah, pretty much.

I didn't want to get hauled off to jail because of some wannabe super-kids, so I made up that sad sack story about my mom and dad being *evil*.

And I *knew* you'd wolf down whatever broken-home bull I fed you.

If I've learned one thing in my long life, it's that angst-ridden brats like you *always* have parent issues.

You're lying. You have some kind of... **hypnotic stare.** That's why we've all been acting so strange around you.

No, you've been acting so strange because you're **teenagers.** You're stupid, predictable, and easy to manipulate.

But **you,** you at least have **spunk.** That's why I'm going to **turn** you... and let you help me kill your **friends.**

No...

Too bad that scary magic wand is still trapped inside your perky little chest, huh? How are you going to **stop** me?

More importantly, why would you **want** to? I mean, I can give you **immortality.**

Besides, it doesn't look like you spend much time in the **sun** as is.

I... I don't want to be **evil.**

Becoming a vampire doesn't change who you are.

Growing up does that, letting the naïveté of adolescence be washed away by the cold hard water of life.

Trust me, when you've seen as much of "humanity" in action as I have, you start to realize that we're all just a bunch of animals.

And that means it's eat... or be eaten.

Someday, you'll understand.

When blood is shed...

...let the Staff of One emerge!

SHUNK!

AHHHHH!

OWW!

Man... will you look at that. It went clean through me and out the other side!

But...

Sorry, kid. Whedon got it wrong.

Stakes don't kill vampires, they just give us *heartburn*.

And what do you know, I'm already on the mend.

See, the only thing that can off me is *sunlight*... and unfortunately for you, that's about three hours away.

Hey, Toph!

I'm sorry, I... I came looking for you because I was *jealous,* and I know it was wrong but I--

I love you!

I love you, too. Can you walk?

No, I can *run.* Come on!

Hurry! He heals fast!

So Topher's a... a *vampire?*

Vampires are *real?*

Unless we're all having the exact same *nightmare...*

"The Hostel"
3:14 A.M.

ZZZZZZ...

Chase, Molly, Gert, *wake up!*

We have to get out of here!

Perfect. It took me *four days* to finally fall asleep...

If this is some kinda *drill*, someone's gonna get *punched*.

Where's Karolina?

Still upstairs, I guess. Why, what's going on?

It's Topher. He's a... a monster. *Literally.*

Say what? He's part of *The Pride?*

No, I don't think he works for our parents, but he's bad. *Very* bad.

I knew it. Old Lace smelled something funny on that guy the second he set foot in here.

RRRRRRR

Well, look who came crawling back.

Topher, it doesn't have to be like--

You forgot to fetch your *stick*, dog.

THWACK

NO!

Are you really surprised to see me, Alex?

Did you honestly think a little *fire* was going to slow me down?

Old Lace.

SIC HIM.

No need to play possum with this thing anymore, huh?

I've already learned all of your *weaknesses.*

Hup!

Uhf!

Hey, Gert? Do you know what really killed all the dinosaurs?

Me neither.

But I bet it sounded something like...

...this!

KERRUNCH

AHNNNN!

Ah yes, your empathic connection.

Lucky you, I forget what it's like to actually *feel* for another life...

Oh, God. **Molly.**

You... you were *awake* for that?

I thought I heard people fighting and... and then I woke up, and then Topher was kissing Lucy in the Sky's neck and then... and then...

Shh, it was just a dream, okay?

I miss my mom and dad!

I... I want my mommy and daddy!

I know, Molly.

I know...

NYARRRGH!

I can't believe you hell creatures were idiotic enough to steal from establishments on *our* turf.

Please, we... we told you, we don't know *where* your kids are!

They took off with The One Who Fathered Us!

The other vampire? He's with our *children*?

He... he *was*. Topher was *slain* last evening. We... we can *sense* when we lose one of our bloodline.

They're telling the truth, Dale.

Fine.

End it, Mr. Minoru.

With pleasure.

NOOOOOO!

Is it possible? Could our offspring have *murdered* one of these things?

You feeling it, too?

Indeed...

Pride.

But don't confuse us with the *junkies* you deal with every night, Lieutenant Flores.

The experimental pharmaceuticals that gave us our powers over light and darkness were *forced* on us by evil men...

Lowlifes who preyed on the fact that me and Cloak were helpless little runaways.

Since that day, Dagger and I have vowed to help *all* children in need.

Swell, 'cause we could sure use a hand finding a few *runaways* of our own.

And I assure you, Dagger and I would not have come to your wretched city if we did not feel strongly about this case.

Please... I wouldn't have asked you two to travel all the way from New York if I didn't think you were the Hayes girl's last hope.

Don't mind Cloak.

East Coast/Left Coast rivalries die hard.

So, ah, what happens now?

We do what we do, Lieutenant.

...we'll call you.

Don't call us...

BEEEEEP BOP

TIEMNS

Calling....

Mr. Wilder?

Yes, I have good news, sire. The Pride may be one step closer to having its *offspring* back...

Well, *this* bites.

Keep it down, Chase. I'm a few chapters away from deciphering the *origin* of The Pride. That might help us figure out what their *next* move will be.

So what, Alex? Even if you *do* decode our parents' big book of evil, it's not like we're gonna be able to *stop* them.

Yeah, *they're* twelve of the most dangerous super-villains on the planet, and *we* almost got decimated by a sixteen-year-old *kid*.

He wasn't a kid.

He was a *monster*.

Whatever! I'm sick and tired of moping around this dump! We have all of this... this *power*. We should be doing something with it, something *good*!

Yeah, like freeing all the turtles at Sea World...

The kid's got a point.

I'm not sure Old Lace and I could survive any more *ampires-vay*.

one and one for whatever then.

Fine, you can tag along, Molly, but under *no circumstances* will you be permitted to leave the van. Got it?

Yes!

We finally get to wear our costumes!

I'm the only one who made a costume?

Thank you, sire. I apologize for interrupting your gathering, but I didn't want to risk sharing this development over an open line.

I believe most of you are familiar with Lieutenant Flores, one of our operatives in the *LAPD*.

I was watching the surveillance tape of your children trying to stop that convenience store robbery a while back, and I got to thinking--

Do any of you earthlings ever get to the *point*?

I got to *thinking,* what's the best way to find a bunch of missing teenage do-gooders?

With *other* runaway super heroes, right? Takes a thief to catch a thief, and all that.

So I had a pal in the NYPD put me in touch with these *Cloak and Dagger* characters, and--

You brought vigilantes?

To *our* town?

Heh. "Stark Naked". We should get some kinda *award* for this.

Finally... a crime in progress.

What, defacing an ad for some evil corporation that's in bed with the military industrial complex? That's not a crime, it's a *public service.*

Come on, Arsenic! This is the first action we've seen all night. We're gonna run outta *gas* before we find something better to fight!

Knock yourself out, Talkback, but I'm not going to help you guys play *junior fascists.*

Should I put my costume on *now,* Lucy in the Sky?

Um, sure, Bruiser... as long as you promise to stay in here and help Arsenic and Old Lace guard our wheels, okay?

Awwww, what a *rip!*

Quiet, team. Let's get into character.

Who's to blame for this, Tandy?

For what?

Children killing children. Every year, it feels as if we see more and more of it.

I don't know, Ty.

But kids have been doing awful things to each other since the *Children's Crusade,* so maybe it's just...

What is it?

Something caught my eye. A *glimmer.*

How far?

Follow me.

I'll light the way.

Stark... naked! *Get it?* Seriously, *ese*, that is the funniest thing I have ever--

Lose the art supplies, Warhol!

You have five seconds.

What... what *are* you?

Mutantes?

...two... one.

BURST!

AHH!

OYE!

Leave now, or she'll be popping *spleens* instead of paint cans.

Nah, son, the only thing popping 'round here's gonna be a *cap* in your mutie--

What is this, a bad remake of West Side Story?

I hate when people mess with the *classics*.

Capa y Daga!

Don't... don't hurt us, yo.

Piece is just a *water pistol*... see?

Vándalos.

Desaparecer o *sufrir.*

Alex Wilder and Nico Minoru?

You're coming with us.

How... how do you know our names? If you work for our *parents,* you can--

DROP THE WEAPON!

UHN!

Sister Grimm!

Everybody, chill!

I... I read about these two on the Bugle's website. Arm & Hammer or something. They're *good guys,* B-list heroes from New York!

B-List?

"Popularity isn't a concern", huh?

L.S.D., you take tall dark and ugly!

I'll get the chick!

Chase, no!

Flame on, skank!

What did you call me?

Leave us alone!

Your light is my sustenance, girl.

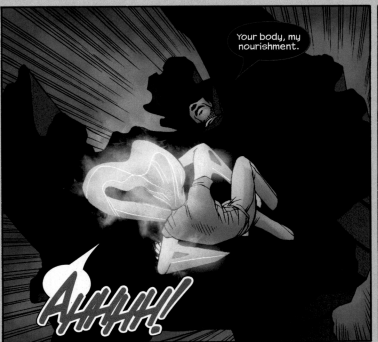

Your body, my nourishment.

AHHHH!

Hope you saved room for seconds, partner.

It's so... so *cold!*

Alex, help m--

Stop it!

I don't know what you've been told, but it's *wrong!* We're not killers, we're... we're just like you!

Tell it to Judge Ito, Wilder.

Don't you see what this is? Two groups of super heroes meet, have a stupid misunderstanding, then fight?

This routine was old when we were *born!* We don't have to--

Be silent, murderer... and enter the fold.

Nice. We didn't take down *Stilt Man* that fast.

Hn.

Uh-oh, I don't like the sound of *that* grunt.

My relationship with the *Darkforce Dimension* has been... *temperamental* since my original abilities were restored during our misadventure in *Cleveland.*

Still, the four within my cloak's shadowy realm... I sense no stain of *blood* on their souls.

What are you saying? They're *not* murderers?

It is possible.

And yet, in one of them, I do recognize a powerful *darkness,* a--

Hey, Desdemona!

What the--?

Huh.

You know, it says a lot about my life that this *isn't* the strangest thing I've ever seen.

Old Lace, *now!*

RAAAARR

Thanks for the cover, O.L.

Is... is she *okay?*

Yeah, just *hungry.*

Um, *problem.*

My powers, they don't have any effect on animals or--

THWAP

Dagger!

UHN!

Easy, Old Lace. She's just a skinny little thing.

We don't want to break her in *two...*

Child, if you have harmed her in any way, I will kill you with my own--

STOP FIGHTING!

Just let our friends out of your ugly *cape!*

Come on, I don't wanna have to rip up your bed sheets!

This is not a "sheet", girl. It is a *cloak*, a gateway to another realm permanently bonded to my very being.

Not even a *god* has the strength to rend it from my--

UMPH!

RAHHHH!

TY!

UHN!

Puh-puh-**please**.

Guh-guh-give it buh-buh-**back** to me.

I'm sorry! I thought you were another **monster**.

I didn't know you were a **stutterer**.

You made me ruh-ruh-**revert** to who I was when I fuh-fuh-**first** donned my cloak.

My mommy is a speech therapist. Maybe *she* can help you!

Bruiser, your parents are psychotic *super-villains*.

Oh, yeah.

I keep forgetting...

Super-villains? What are you two *talking* about?

Yeah, our *folks*. The people who duped you into coming after us.

No, the *police* asked for our help.

Same diff. They're all in it together, part of something called "The Pride". They murdered a chick and framed *us* for the crime.

But the little girl you guys *kidnapped*...

How blonde *are* you? *That's* Molly Hayes!

Aww! You ruined my secret identity!

See, we didn't *kidnap* anybody. We *rescued* her.

Oh, my God. Then your pals... *they're* innocent, too?

And now they're tr-tr-trapped in the Duh-Duh-Darkforce Dimension.

The *where* now?

What do you mean they're *lost?!*

When Molly ruh-ruh-ripped my cloak from me, she suh-suh-severed my connection to your friends.

It was an accident! I didn't know it was a *magic* cape!

Hold on, I have to wrap my brain around this.

This guy's outfit is like the mystical equivalent of a portal to the internet, but the server crashed, so before we can perform a *search,* we have to find a way to get it back online... *right?*

That was the worst analogy I've ever heard... but it gives me an idea.

My light daggers have a *purifying* quality. If I pump Ty full of them, I might be able to *repair* his link to Creepsville.

There's a duh-duh-danger of *overdose,* but it's our only huh-huh-*hope.*

Close your eyes, kiddies.

This is gonna be bright...

...but it might not be *pretty.*

GAH!

NYARRGH!

OOF!

Presto!

Everybody... in one... *piece?*

You. You sent us to *Hell.*

Hands off, Talkback.

We don't need any more meaningless punching.

Yeah, then what *do* we need?

The only thing our kind dreads...

Dialogue.

Twenty-nine Minutes Later...

So this Lieutenant Flores jerk who put us on your scent...?

Yeah, sounds like he's an agent of The Pride, too. I'm sorry, they've got their fingers in *everything.*

We want our parents taken down *hard* for what they've done, but obviously, we're not quite Earth's Mightiest Heroes yet.

Speaking of which, I'm good friends with the Black Widow.

I'm sure she could put you in touch with Captain America and those guys, maybe send *them* out here to clean house.

Are... are you serious? That would be *amazing!*

In the meantime, you children are clearly not safe in Los Angeles. You will come back to New York with us.

In *that* thing? No offense, bro, but I'd sooner spend the night at Neverland Ranch.

I'm ashamed how often I agree with Chase, but I don't think I could survive another trip like that either.

Well, maybe we can stay in L.A. for a *little* longer, Nico... until the good guys are ready to pick us up in a Quinjet or whatever?

Pick you up *where*, exactly?

No way, sister! The last time we told someone about my hideout, they nearly *ate* us!

Chase, these guys are *heroes*.

So were my mom and pops, up until I found out they *weren't*.

Seriously, we don't know these cats from--

Enough. Cloak and Dagger have all the info they need to send the super-people after our parents.

They can assemble a posse in Manhattan, and we'll go back into hiding until our 'rents are in the slammer and the coast is clear.

Maybe that makes us cowards... but I *love* that plan. I don't think I have any fight left in me.

Hey, you guys are *anything* but cowards.

Me and Cloak didn't have *half* your guts and street smarts when *we* ran away from home.

Hn.

Well, I guess we should head back to our... place. Can we give you a ride somewhere or--

Thanks, Alex, but I think we'll rest here until we've gotten enough juice back for our jump to NYC.

You just keep taking good care of your team, okay?

Hang in there, Molly! This is all gonna be over soon!

Thanks!

It was awesome to meet you, Cloak and Dazzler!

My *name* is...

I hate this city.

UCLA Medical Center
1:34 A.M.

Unknown Caller

BZZBZZBZZ

What?

Lieutenant Flores?

Speak up, kid. You're mumbling. I can barely understand--

You're the dork who sent Cloak and Dagger after us, right? I'm surprised our parents haven't *killed* you yet.

Who... who *is* this?

Right now, I'm the only friend you've got.

You're one of their **children**, aren't you?

The Pride told me they might have a **mole** in your gang, but I didn't believe--

Quiet. I don't have long. I'm at a payphone outside some taco shack, and the others think I'm in the bathroom.

What do you--

Listen, Cloak and Dagger are on a rooftop in Van Nuys, but I'm not sure how much longer they'll be there.

Lieutenant, they **know** about The Pride.

How?

Doesn't matter. The only thing **you** should care about is cleaning up your mess.

But I'm stuck in the hospital! The Pride shot my **kneecap** off!

Do **something**... or the next bullet will probably be to your **brain**.

LA MEDIC
24 HOURS

Are you strong enough for the journey home now, Tandy?

I am if you are.

I feel terrible for dragging you out here. I was easily duped by the kind of authority you and I used to always *question.*

Don't beat yourself up, Ty. We both made mistakes...

...but maybe something *good* will come from--

KASCHOWW

Leave it to Stein to suggest *experimentation.* Still, I have no qualms, so long as it's just on *humans...*

Hold them steady, Frank. If we cause one incorrect synapse to fire, we could lobotomize them both.

On my count, dear. One, two...

AHHHHHH!

Are they...?

No. Merely unconscious. I believe we have... *success.*

They'll wake up confused and disoriented, but they shouldn't remember anything from the last twenty-four hours.

I'll plant a suggestion in their subconscious to make them attribute the blackout to *binge drinking.* That should confuse the little teetotalers...

We haven't cut it that close since the *Wonder Man* incident a few years back. We're just lucky our *"deep throat"* called when he... or *she* did.

I still don't get it. If one of our runaways is really *loyal* to us, why not call us *directly?* Or at least tell us where they are?

Yes, who in *God's* name is our mole...?

The Pride's evil cookbook?

It's more than that, Nico. It's a history of their whole twisted organization.

I haven't totally mastered the *Decoder Ring* we stole from Karolina's mom, but I've been able to roughly translate the first few chapters or so.

And? How does it start?

How else, Gert?

"In the beginning..."

Los Angeles, California Twenty Years Ago.

Eat lead, pigs!

Baby, you are my *hero!*

So you don't believe what your Ma said? About me not being "marriage material"?

You *know* I'm glad we eloped, Geoff. Someday, the two of us are gonna *own* this town, just like--

Geoffrey and Catherine Wilder, you have been *summoned.*

FWASH

You worthless *meshuggener!*

You've stranded us in the 1980s!

Have you ever even *read* a history book? This is the worst decade of the millennium!

Relax, Stacey. Just a minor misalignment in our 4-D portico. I'll have us up and running again in no time.

ELECTRIC BOOGALOO

"No time" is what I'm concerned about, you piece of *shock!* We have to get these stolen artifacts back to last century before--

Dale and Stacey Yorkes, you have been *summoned.*

FWASH

MUTIE SCUM!

No! *Please!* My husband and I have been *good neighbors* to you people! We're not--

Stop whimpering, Alice! I'm tired of this!

Let's show these man-apes what *evolution* looks--

Gene and Alice Hayes, you have been *summoned.*

FWASH

Victor and Janet Stein, you have been *summoned.*

Robert and Tina Minoru, you have been *summoned.*

Frank and Leslie Dean, you have been *summoned.*

Guess again, you community theater rejects.

My husband and I aren't *freaks.*

I beg your *pardon!* If you bigots have a problem with Homo superior--

I don't know why you deviants kidnapped us from our own *wedding...* but you made a huge mistake.

My bride and I may only *dabble* in the black arts, but we have more than enough power to defeat *you.*

What are you *talking* about? Gene and I had nothing to do with--

Rik hr Nisanti!

AHHH!

CREATURES, BE *GONE!*

PAFT

THE REST OF YOU, BE *SILENT.*

WE ARE THE ONES WHO CALLED YOU HERE, TO OUR *VIVARIUM* BENEATH THE SEAS...

Whoa! Back up... the *whozit?*

I think that's Hebrew for "mighty men", um... *heroes.*

The Gibborim are also mythical *evil giants,* who supposedly predate the Old Testament.

I can't remember if they're related to Nephilim, but I'm pretty sure they had six fingers on each hand and six toes on each...

What?

I like books about monsters. Sue me...

So you're saying our parents are somehow connected to a bunch of ancient, super-sized, fantasy creatures with deformed extremities?

Well, that would explain the *six* little piggies on the cover of the Abstract.

You know, the more I find out about our 'rents, the more I wish I was *adopted.*

This is worse than the time I accidentally *walked in* on them.

You guys seriously think this Neverending Story is *real?* I mean, I can almost accept *vampires,* and maybe even *Martians,* like Karolina...

...but giants? That's *impossible!*

Hey, I'm not from--

Funny, that's exactly what your *dad* said...

Colonists? From *where*?

None of your business, "wise man".

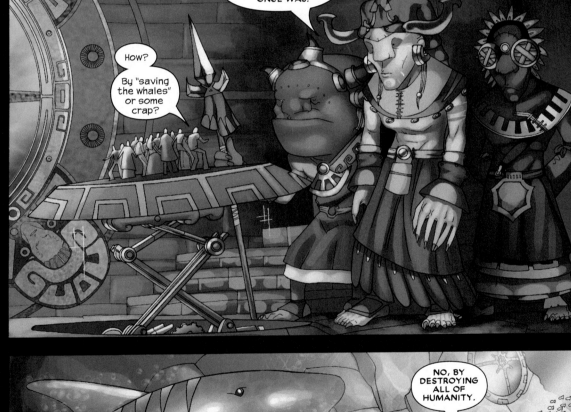

WITH YOUR HELP, WE WILL RESTORE EARTH TO THE GLORIOUS PARADISE IT ONCE WAS.

How? By "saving the whales" or some crap?

NO, BY DESTROYING ALL OF HUMANITY.

What?

Intriguing.

But what's in it for us... other than the *usual* entertainment value of wasting Earthlings, of course?

THE GIBBORIM WILL AUGMENT EACH OF YOUR ABILITIES, GIVE YOU ENOUGH POWER TO CLAIM DOMINION OVER THE ENTIRE CITY OF ANGELS... AND BEYOND.

What good is world dominance if there's not a *world* left to dominate?

IT WILL TAKE A QUARTER-CENTURY FOR YOU TO SUPPLY THE GIBBORIM WITH ALL THAT WE NEED TO RESHAPE THIS ONCE-PRISTINE ORB.

UNTIL THEN, IT SHALL BE YOUR KINGDOM TO DO WITH AS YOU PLEASE.

And when our twenty-five years are up?

SIX OF YOU WILL BE PERMITTED TO JOIN US IN OUR NEW EDEN, WHERE YOU WILL BE GRANTED *ETERNAL LIFE.*

THE OTHER SIX SHALL *PERISH* WITH THE REST OF YOUR MISERABLE RACE.

That's insane!

NO, IT IS *INCENTIVE.* THE REWARD SHALL GO TO THE SIX APOSTLES WHO SERVE US MOST FAITHFULLY.

Why should we trust you? When we're done "serving", how do we know you won't just say "fee fi fo fum" and slaughter the lot of us?

TOMORROW IS ALWAYS UNCERTAIN, AS YOU WELL KNOW, TRAVELER, BUT THE POWER WE CAN GIVE YOU TODAY IS NOT.

STILL, YOU ARE WELCOME TO DECLINE OUR OFFER AND RETURN TO YOUR LIVES OF QUIET DESPERATION. NONE OF YOU WILL BE DIFFICULT TO REPLACE.

Twenty-five years of guaranteed power... plus a fifty-fifty shot at immortality? I don't think we can afford to say no, Catherine.

Geoff, we're talking about the end of mankind! My *mother...*

...will be *long gone* by the time any of this goes down.

And so will the *rest* of the planet if Reagan keeps playing his games. The way I see it, we're just lining up on the right side of the *inevitable.*

If we agree to your terms, you creatures said that you'll need us to *supply* you with something... but *what?*

THE TWELVE OF YOU WILL GATHER ONCE A YEAR FOR THE RITE OF BLOOD...

If the Gibborim select Victor and me for paradise, I intend to give my spot to our *offspring*.

I told you, I have no interest in living forever *without* you.

That's so... *romantic*.

Actually, Stacey and I had *also* been talking about a baby.

The little lady's biological clock is ticking, and that's one bit of time I can't seem to get around.

Oh, Robert, could *we*?

But our shot at *eternal glory*...

We're *already* getting twenty-five years of heaven and more wealth and power than we ever imagined. What more do the two of us need?

Hmm. We never had a way of knowing which six of us the Gibborim would select for immortality, but if *each* couple donated their place to a single child...

You're out of your *mind*, Wilder! I don't even *want* a kid!

Besides, it's not fair! Because of our mutant genes, my husband and I might not be *able* to conceive.

When the twelve of us agreed to go on this journey, we vowed to walk every last step *together*.

Are you *in*... or are you *out*?

Think about it, friends. If we proceed as planned, there's no guarantee that any of you will live past the Final Wave.

But if we all promise to give our chance at the next world to an *heir*, the legacy of the entire Pride will be assured.

...

I'll *think* about it. A baby would probably get me on the cover of *People*, I suppose.

It may take *time*... but we're certainly willing to try.

We'll tell our children what gift awaits them after they turn *eighteen*, just before the end.

Until then, they need never know just how much we *sacrificed* on their behalf...

Oh, my God.

All the horrible things our parents have done... they did them for *us*.

Figures. The previous generation is *always* screwing up the world in the name of helping out the next one.

Are we gonna have to do a book report on this, or can we just skip to the *end* already?

The cover of *People*...?

I'm with Molly. What more do we need to hear?

If all that stuff is true, it's more than enough evidence to put our parents away for life, right? We've gotta *show* this to somebody!

Like *who*, Chase? The LAPD is on our parents' *payroll*, remember?

Yeah...

The twelve of us joined The Pride because we each wanted one of the Gibborim's six tickets to paradise for *ourselves*.

We *never* would have given up that shot at eternal life if my wife hadn't become *pregnant*... if *all* of us hadn't decided that we needed *little ones* to share our empty mansions with.

But it was *years* ago that we agreed to donate our chance at immortality to those six kids. Back then, none of us imagined that we would ever *want* to live forever.

Surviving to an age like *forty* sounded like an eternity already, more than enough time to enjoy all the Gibborim had granted us.

But now we're *old men*, rapidly approaching the Final Wave, and the ungrateful brats we sacrificed everything for have *abandoned* us.

Admit it, some nights, you think about *letting* your son perish with the rest of this wretched populace... and taking his spot in the Next World for *yourself*.

NEVER!

⋛hkk⋚

NO!

Chase, lay down some suppressive fire!

I have no clue what that means...

...but this is for *Rodney King*, y'all!

FWOOOM

What did you do to my *hideout*, Teen Witch?

I'm sorry, Chase!

I... I just wanted a little *tremor*, but I can't shut it off!

Karolina, use your E.T. powers to blast us another exit!

Alex, I can't! I'm not that strong!

You *have* to be! You--

Um, gang?

Either I'm getting *taller*, or the ceiling's getting--

KRAKADOOM

We're... we're *alive?*

Yeah, awesome. Too bad we're surrounded by a *mountain.*

I wonder if asphyxiation is worse than getting *crushed* to death...?

Karolina, can you push this stuff *off* of us?

I... I don't think so. Taking everything I've got... just to hold it *up.*

It's not *fair!*

This place was so cool, but now it *stinks.*

I had to leave my old house, and now I'm gonna have to leave *this* one?

It's not *fair!*

KRAK!

"...we run."

Well? What do you have, Victor?

The good news is they're not *dead.*

The bad news is they're not *here.* My readings suggest that all six of our children burrowed free and *retreated* about forty minutes ago.

Then they couldn't have gotten far...

...which is exactly why we should leave the hunt to our *boys in blue.* The two of us can't afford to be seen "in character" by people *not* on The Pride's payroll.

Besides, we have to meet the others for the Rite of Thunder in just a few hours. The Gibborim will *vaporize* us if we don't show.

You expect me to leave my son to *these* incompetents? They nearly killed him *once!*

Geoffrey, at least they smoked them out. It's only a matter of time before--

We got one!

Is she *still* asleep?

What do you think, Talkback?

Molly practically dug us all the way to *China.*

I wish. We covered some good ground tonight...

HOLLYWOOD

...but not *enough.*

The Dean Residence
7:30 P.M.

IDIOTS!

Wilder and Stein *had* them, and they let our children *slip away!*

Use your inside voice, dear. You heard what Victor said, they were tipped off by whichever child is our *mole.*

It's only a matter of time before he or she alerts us to their *new* whereabouts.

KRUNCH

Indeed. I trust we'll hear from *Molly* again soon enough.

15

**Wilder Family Private Beach
Malibu, California
8:08 P.M.**

What the devil is taking them so long?

Don't get your spacesuit in a bunch, Mrs. Dean. They'll *be* here.

When? The last time we were late, the Gibborim threatened to send us to--

Calm yourself, Leslie.

The gang's all here.

After you, Tina.

Hnn.

Do you have any clue what Minoru was talking about? Saying one of *us* might be a mole to our *kids*?

Of course not. I'm just thankful he's *suspicious* about *that,* and not the fact he and the rest of The Pride are about to be *executed* by us.

You sure you want to go through with this *tonight,* Leslie? I don't want to throw away *two years* worth of planning, but our girls are still--

They'll turn up, Alice. But right now is the *perfect* time for our two families to seize eternal glory for ourselves.

The humans' minds are with their children, and their armaments are in their homes.

Believe me, I've thought of *everything.*

Sorry, I just wanted one more before--

Me, too.

And what I tried to tell you when we were trapped inside Cloak the other night--

I *know*, Alex.

No, you really don't.

I wanted to tell you-- *all* of you-- that no matter how I ever acted, I always secretly *looked forward* to those get-togethers our parents made us have.

Most of my "friends" were just Xbox screennames, but I really liked you guys. Even before all this. I always felt, like, a *connection* to...

Whatever, I don't believe *any* of you would ever betray what we have here, but if you try... the rest of us won't hesitate to *destroy* you. Agreed?

Agreed.

Totally.

Yeah. Ditto.

Here we go again.

"Suffer the children..."

Whoa... *jellyfishes.*

Quiet, Molly.

Let's let Nico concentrate, okay?

It's fine, Karolina. The Staff of One is doing all the heavy lifting.

Besides, I think it *likes* when you guys talk.

Then, um... what's everyone wanna be when they grow up?

Assuming we live through this, I mean.

The Marine Vivarium
10:51 P.M.

PLOP

Is... is this *Atlantis?*

I don't know, but it's *huge.*

Come on, we've got about a thirty-minute walk until we hit the Gibborim's master chamber...

PLOP

Is... is this
Atlantis?

I don't
know, but it's
huge.

Come on,
we've got about
a thirty-minute
walk until we hit the
Gibborim's master
chamber...

AFFIRMATIVE.

SENTRY... POWERING... DOWN...

Gah. Why do they always hit *me* first?

Alex, how did you...?

Philoprogenitiveness, the love of parent for child!

I guess The Pride finally found a better password than "password". My decoder ring usually has trouble with anything longer than three syllables, but I was able to--

GUYS!

It's Chase.

He... he isn't breathing.

16

Alex, if one of us really *is* loyal to The Pride, *Karolina* might be the mole. What if she's trying to *hurt* Chase, or--

Forget that!

Just... try CPR first, Gert. If that doesn't work--

I'll do what I can, but health class was *three semesters* ago.

Gert, listen to me! Dr. Heimlich says--

Two breaths, now check for pulse, right?

Don't use your thumb! It's got its own heartbeat in it!

I'm serious, I'm pretty sure this is *wrong!*

I was reventilating him.

Anyone who says otherwise gets fed to my %@#ing dinosaur.

What's everybody moping around for?

Let's go kick some--

Whoa.

Bed... totally... *spinning...*

Chase, you're in no condition to take on The Pride.

You already died *once.* We shouldn't push our luck.

I'm so sorry, guys. I... I really screwed up.

You're a *hero,* you moron. That monster would have pounded Old Lace and me into fossils if you hadn't stepped in.

Well, now I'm just *deadweight.*

You dudes gotta press on without me.

We can't just leave Chase here by himself!

He'll be fine, Karolina. I already used the Abstract to deactivate all of the main foyer's defense systems.

Besides, without Chase's firepower, we're gonna need the rest of the team more than ever.

You ain't without *nothin',* Alex.

Here, I want you to take my x-ray specs and these Fistigon things...

Chase, I...
I *can't.*

Bro, all you've got is a *book.* How do you plan to fight our parents? With *literacy?*

Trust me, you've earned a power-up.

I don't even know how to *use* this stuff!

If *I* could figure it out, a geek like you should be able to master 'em in no time flat.

And Nico, take my switchblade, so you can pick that oversized *splinter* out of your soul.

Thanks, Chase. For *everything.* We'll come back for you as soon as we're done rocking the hand that rocks the cradle.

Just teach my folks a lesson, okay?

Say no more.

Do you ever have second thoughts, Stacey?

Since when is the "dark sorcerer" uncomfortable with a little black magic?

It's not just the Rite of Thunder. My heart hardened to these unholy ceremonies years ago. I'm talking about what they're meant to *accomplish.*

Are you still willing to help *destroy* the entire planet?

Oh, *heavens,* yes. Before my dolt of a husband totaled our 4-D portico *permanently,* we visited *thousands* of possible futures, each worse than the last.

And all of these timelines were overrun with the same wretched thing: *super heroes.*

The X-Men, the Avengers, the Fantastic bloody Four... their kind dominated every era, ensuring that people like *us* never challenged the mundane status quo.

Believe me, a world filled with fifty-year-old men punching one another is no place for children.

The next generation deserves something *new*... and that's exactly what

Float on.

Put us *down*, young lady!

And tell us what you've done with our *son!*

Chase is fine, Mrs. Stein.

No thanks to y--

Time out!

SVASH

Wha... what happened?

I've got to give you credit, Nico. You always made using this thing look *easy*.

I had to try a zillion different phrases before the Staff of One finally *unfroze* you from that *Girl, Interrupted* spell your mom and dad--

Alex, *look out!*

Your parents are right behind you!

I know.

They always have been.

Gert, Molly... *Karolina!*

Don't worry, they're just *unconscious*, like most of The Pride.

I needed the other kids out of the picture, but I wasn't about to let them be *killed*... unless I ran out of options, of course.

No.

No, not you.

You... you *can't* be the traitor.

You have to *betray* something to be a traitor, Nico. And I've never been anything but *loyal* to the people who matter.

I just explained everything to my mom and dad, but I'd be happy to fill *you* in, too.

This is all just a... a *trick*, right? You're lulling The Pride into a false sense of security before you spring your master--

Remember that secret passageway in my parents' house? You know how I said I found it a few months ago, when I was snooping for Christmas presents?

Well, that wasn't *exactly* true...

"I actually discovered it more than a *year* ago, at one of our families' annual get-togethers."

Holy...

"The grown-ups were having their 'charity meeting' in the basement, and you guys were engrossed in some stupid movie, so I decided to *explore.*"

Would someone please remind me why I'm missing lacrosse finals for this *lamefest?*

Have you ever thought about getting *contacts,* Nico?

Well...

Hey, Gert, do stuffed animals go to heaven when they die? Or hell?

"At the end of that long corridor, from the other side of that one-way mirror, I saw our parents dressed in their costumes. Obviously, I was *freaked*..."

"...but not nearly as freaked as I was when I saw them *kill* someone, in the same ceremony *you* saw a year later."

But instead of calling the cops, I kept my *mouth shut,* and gave the people who raised me the benefit of the doubt.

I knew there had to be a logical explanation for what I had seen... and I was *right.*

Alex, honey, maybe you should *ease* Nico into--

"I spent the next few nights sneaking into my dad's subbasement after he went to bed. I read as much as I could decipher about The Pride and their history.

"I learned about the *Gibborim,* and what our parents sacrificed to make this world a better place for the six of us.

"I couldn't believe it... my mom and dad were *heroes.*"

Are you *insane?* Alex, you saw them *murder* an innocent girl!

They *had* to, Nico! You've seen *Wrath of Khan,* right? "The good of the many outweighs the good of the one!"

"Anyway, I discovered pretty quickly that not *everyone* in The Pride was as noble as *my* parents..."

You're *certain* the Wilders are asleep?

They won't be if you keep *yammering*, woman.

I'm still not sure I completely understand what we're--

Dr. Hayes, for the last time, the copy of the Abstract that the Gibborim gave each of us details the past *and* future of The Pride.

The mere act of *thinking* the plan we just conceived means that it will now be in the book. We have to destroy those pages before the others read them.

But Mr. Dean, if the Abstract can chronicle what hasn't even happened yet, wouldn't our future misdeeds have been in there from the very *beginning*?

It's magic, mutant.

If you think about it too hard, your *brain* will explode.

Hurry up with that *decoder ring*. We still have to find and alter three more tomes before the night is through.

But if the Wilders notice the missing passages... if they suspect that we're preparing to *murder* the rest of The Pride at next year's Rite of Thunder--

--you and I will know the second we read their thoughts, dear, and *lobotomize* them before they ever have a chance to tell anyone.

After all, Alex's parents are *powerless*. It's the *others* we have to worry about...

Molly and Karolina's parents were plotting to *kill* our folks, Nico, so their families could have the six spots in the next world meant for us kids.

I wanted to warn my mom and dad, but I couldn't do it without putting their lives in danger.

No. You... you wanted your parents to be *arrested*. You said--

I had to say a *lot* of things, Nico. I'm sorry, but I knew I couldn't stop this *coup* without *help*.

So when I read about weapons and resources hidden in each of your homes--

Wait, *that's* why you made us sneak back into our houses after we ran away? You said you were looking for *evidence* to use against The Pride, but you were really--

--collecting my arsenal, *and* unlocking some of my soldiers' powers.

What, you thought it was just a *coincidence* that we stumbled onto fire gauntlets and... and telepathic *dinosaurs*?

This has all been part of some sick *plan*?

Oh, not all of it. I've made a few mistakes along the way. I never would have invited that vampire back to the Hostel if I had known he was going to *kiss* you. Still, I had to find *some* way to toughen you guys up for this battle.

That's impossible! It... it was *my* idea to take on The Pride at the Rite of Thunder!

You didn't have a choice, Nico. Not after I led the police to our *hideout*.

Rule number one of gaming: a good dungeon master always makes his players feel like *they're* in control, especially when they're *not*.

God, Alex, this isn't a *game!*

And you weren't just a *pawn.* I... I *love* you. That's why I've decided to let you come along.

Come along *where?*

To eternal paradise, Nico, *with* your parents.

In light of recent events, Mr. Wilder and I have been forced to... *amend* our agreement with the rest of The Pride.

Everything's going to be fine, sweetie. Our two families will finish off our betrayers before the Gibborim arrive at midnight.

After we feed the giants the young woman's *soul* we collected at the last Rite of Blood, the Gibborim will undoubtedly award immortality to the six of *us.*

And then what? They blow up the rest of the *world?!*

Nico, remember what we talked about? Before our first kiss? How it felt like people had screwed up the planet beyond repair, and there was nothing kids like us could do about it?

Well, now we can! We can hit the reset button on the whole world, remake it the way it's *supposed* to be. You and me, and maybe someday... *our* kids.

Bruiser's mom broke my glasses, but she forgot to break my *brain.*

Old Lace... *fetch.*

Hey...!

Good girl.

Give up, Alex.

Don't make me *demonstrate* how much better than you I am with this thing.

Try it, and "Lucy in the Sky" goes up in *smoke.*

Sorry, got tired of waiting for you dudes, so I hot-wired Frogger here.

What I miss?

Chase?
But I... I made sure you were too *hurt* to fight. I--

AAAAHH!

HANDS OFF!

That's *enough*, young lady!

Alex has given our family an amazing gift, and you will *show* him your appreciation.

Gift?

What kind of shanghai *is* this, Wilder?

You Benedict Arnolds were going to steal *our* children's place in the Afterworld? After everything we've done together?

If that's true, I'm gonna rip your lying head from your--

Stop fighting!

Molly?

Molly, precious, please... *please* be careful with that.

It... it has a little girl's *spirit* in it.

NOOOO!

THE RITE OF THUNDER HAS FAILED. YOUR SELFISH DEDICATION TO YOUR PROGENY HAS REDUCED DECADES OF SERVICE TO *NOTHINGNESS.*

THEREFORE, WE SHALL USE WHAT POWER WE HAVE LEFT TO *END* THE LIVES OF YOU *AND* YOUR CHILDREN.

KAZZOW

AHHH!

Nico, get out of here! Your father and I will try to hold them off!

No! I won't let them butcher you! I don't care what you've done, I--

I am still your mother, and you will do as I *say!*

Sister Grimm, please!

We... we have to take care of each other now!

So *this* is what we're reduced to, eh, mother?

Yes, love... empty nesters.

Gert, what... what happened to *Alex*? Those things just--

We'll explain topside! Right now, we've gotta *jet*. Do you know how to pilot this thing?

If by pilot you mean "smash through stuff", then...

...sorta.

POOM!

REEBIT

Did... did I kill anybody?

Molly slept through the whole ride. We're *fine*.

Well, you land better than you *kiss*, Chase.

It's over. I can't believe it's actually--

Excuse me...

I'm Chester Biloxi, and that's the question six area teenagers recently had to ask themselves... and it's what we'll be talking about today on "Tsunami", Los Angeles' most *exciting* news magazine.

As we all know, three months ago, it was revealed that twelve of our city's most prominent socialites were actually part of a villainous secret organization known as *The Pride*.

According to documents obtained by New York-based super-group *The Avengers*, these seemingly normal families had criminal operatives placed throughout business, government, and perhaps most disturbingly, *law enforcement* here in California.

Though The Pride's true agenda remains a mystery, an exhaustive federal investigation has seen scores of corporate CEOs, high-ranking politicians, and even police officers indicted on charges ranging from racketeering to *homicide*.

And while the Avengers have been instrumental in aiding in the systematic dismantlement of this shadowy cabal's far-reaching network of conspirators, they are *not* responsible for the defeat of The Pride themselves.

That honor apparently goes to the six only *children* of these murderous adults, who ran away from home after witnessing their parents *kill* a young girl in some kind of occult ceremony.

In the hopes of learning more about this amazing story, our own Cadie MacDunnough recently caught up with *Captain America* outside of City Hall.

I'm sorry, I got your text message, but I... I was worried it might be a *trap*. I know the judge promised no one would come after us, but--

Tell me about it. I've been having nightmares for *weeks.*

You have any trouble sneaking out?

Are you kidding? I think both of my foster parents are addicted to prescription painkillers. They probably wouldn't notice if I was gone for a *week.*

Least you *found* a family. I'm still trapped at Father Flanagan's Home for Unwanted Goth Kids. I'm pretty sure one of the boys at my shelter is *obsessed* with me, too.

JAMES DEAN

Are you guys, you know... *going together* or whatever?

After what Alex did to me? To *us*?

I've sworn off boys *forever.*

Oh.

Cool.

Anyway, good to see you're doing all right.

Not according to my *social worker*. She's got me going to therapy three times a week.

You and me both. I have to sit in sessions with these kids whose lives were "ruined" because their dads never went to see their Little League games.

How am I supposed to talk about what *we* went through?

I know, there's not exactly a support group for people whose parents got murdered by *giants*, huh? That's sorta why I wanted to see everyone again.

You think they understood my message?

"Meet where we got together the *first* time we ran away?" I can't imagine anyone's forgotten that night, K.

How long have you been coming to this place anyway?

My dad used to take me here when I was little. He was *crazy* about James Dean. I realize now that he and my mom probably took their last name from him... after they came to Earth, you know?

I wonder what they were like back then? If they used to be good people on our... our "home world" or whatever. I wonder what turned them--

Past your curfew, isn't it, girls?

Son of a...

What was *that* for?

My *name* is Arsenic.

What are you *talking* about, psycho? We quit using those stupid codenames *months*--

I thought you were *dead!* I thought you got hit by a bus or... or killed by *drifters* or something. Why didn't you respond to any of my e-mails?

I was *busy!*

Doing *what?*

Looking for your stupid dinosaur, okay? And I *found* her.

You... you did?

Mmf!

Mmmm...

Ick, I forgot about how much freakin' *snogging* you guys do.

"Snogging"? Where the heck did you pick up--

Um, Chase, if you come up for air at some point... could you tell us *where* Old Lace is?

Oh, remember when the Avengers had a West Coast team, back when we were kids? These zoning permits I, uh... *found* showed that they still have a storage facility somewhere on Palos Verdes.

Exact address is classified, but I figure Arsenic's dino-sense will start tingling when we get close.

Then what the hell are we waiting for?

We can't break into a *government facility!* If we get caught stealing, everyone's gonna accuse us of what most people already think... that we're no different than our *parents.*

It's not stealing if it belongs to us! Besides, we *won't* get caught. My Fistigon gloves may be deep-sixed, and our ride might be impounded, but Molly and Karolina are still all Powerpuffed out.

And you've got that *magic stick* up your soul, right? All you have to do is *cut* yourself, and we're ready to rock.

Yeah, but I... I haven't used the Staff of One since--

Please, Sister Grimm. My mom and dad kept Old Lace locked away for *years.*

If we let that happen to her again, how are we any better than them?

Well...

JAMES DEAN

I... I can't.

What are you waiting for, dude? *Cut yourself!*

You gotta release your staff!

Nnnn...

HAA!

KAZAXXXX

CRUNK

Okay, then.

That was officially the third most awesome thing I've ever seen.

We did it! We totally won... and nobody got knocked out or set on fire for once!

And we didn't even need Alex to do it!

We *never* needed Alex. He just tried to keep us down, to make sure that we never became a *real* threat to our 'rents.

One more thing that backstabbing toolbox screwed up.

I found her!

In here! Old Lace is in here!

DEET DOOT

RRRR

I missed you, too, girl.

Way to be, Arsenic!

You... you can call me *Gert*, Chase.

You sure? Even though that's the name your *folks* gave you?

Well... maybe *some* things they gave us are worth holding onto.

I don't want to rain on another parade... but what now?

It's not like Gert can take Old Lace back to her *dorm*.

I'm not *going* back, Nico.

I thought I'd be able to put up with being controlled by know-nothing adults again... but I *can't*. Not after everything we've been through.

I'm with Gert. I want to be *free*. I want to *fly* again.

Can I come, too?

Molly, you've got it great now! You're with kids who're just like you!

They're *nothing* like me, Nico.

The girls I live with are just mutants. You guys are my *friends*.

Listen, this is all very flowery and nice, but if we make a break for it now, *everyone* will be on our tails... cops, child welfare services, the *Avengers*.

What do we do when they come after us?

What do you think, dummy?

"I never thought I'd live to see eighteen."

"Isn't that dumb? Every day, I look in the mirror and say, *What? You still here? Man!*"

Apparently, this thing doesn't fly so much as *jump*, so, uh... hang on to your valuables, ladies.

Vertical thrust in five... four... three...

"Like even today. I woke up this morning, you know? And the sun was shining and everything was nice, and I thought...

"...this is going to be one terrific day, so you better live it up, boy..."

WEEEEE!

"...because tomorrow, maybe you'll be gone."
-James Dean
Rebel Without a Cause

EIGHTEEN

Team Runaways,

Last issue? What do you mean, LAST ISSUE? What the hell does that mean? Did you type it wrong? Were you thinking of something else, like maybe the *Sub-Mariner* or the *Smurfs*? How can there be a last issue when the story is obviously going to continue for years? You're some kind of wrong person. Have it looked into.

Your fan,
Joss Whedon

Yep, that's the real Joss Whedon, of *BUFFY*, *ASTONISHING X-MEN* and, uh, *ROSEANNE* fame. Cool, huh? But thanks to the vocal support of loyal readers like you (and Joss), I am thrilled to announce that this is NOT the last issue of *Runaways*. Our kids are going on a well-deserved vacation for a few short months, but the entire creative team will be bringing them back in early 2005 for *RUNAWAYS #1*! One chapter in the lives of our young heroes has ended, but an all-new, all-different one is about to begin.

THANK YOU NOTE FROM CHRISTINA STRAIN

RUNAWAYS
EXPANDED PROPOSAL
BY BRIAN K. VAUGHAN

At some point in their lives, all young people believe that their parents are the most evil people alive.

But what if they really are?

When six young friends discover that their parents are actually super-villains, the teenagers agree to run away from their respective homes. Using the unique gifts they inherited (or stole) from their immoral mothers and fathers, these fugitive heroes vow to do everything they can to atone for their parents' crimes.

Smallville meets Harry Potter in this all-ages action/adventure series.

THE PREMISE

Alex Wilder always knew that there was something strange about his parents, a happily married couple of wealthy Los Angeles socialites. Instead of family reunions, the Wilders host annual get-togethers with five other families. While the adults discuss their charity program in private, Alex has to hang out with their kids, an oddball collection of five other only children.

At one of these gatherings, the six teenagers make a horrifying discovery. They learn that their parents actually lead something called The Pride, an underworld organization of criminal kingpins, mad scientists, alien warlords, mutant terrorists, tyrannical time-travelers, and dark wizards. Working largely in secret to obtain complete world dominion, these all-new villains make Dr. Doom look like Dr. Evil.

The kids try to tell the authorities what they've learned, but the police are either disbelieving or under the far-reaching influence of the Pride. With no one else to turn to, the six teens agree to run away from their homes, but not before they pilfer strange technology and mystical devices from their corrupt parents.

Now on the run from their enraged families (some of whom want the children killed), the Runaways take up residence in the Hostel, an underground youth hotel buried during a California earthquake. In this unique, totally accessible new corner of the Marvel Universe, the would-be heroes give themselves new names, new attire, and a new purpose... to protect the community, right the wrongs of their parents, and one day bring the Pride to justice.

Still, the fruit usually doesn't fall too far from the tree, and some Runaways will have to fight the temptation to follow in their parents' footsteps. Matters will grow even more complicated when it becomes apparent that one of the Runaways may actually be a mole, loyal to the lethal Pride.

THE CHARACTERS

Wilder - The oldest of the Runaways, Alex Wilder is a seventeen-year-old African-American male. Though he has no powers, Wilder is a brilliant young strategist with a passion for directors like Hitchcock and online games like EverQuest. Now co-leader of the Runaways, Wilder is ashamed that his role-model parents are actually two criminal kingpins who fund the Pride's terrorist activities, and he intends to do whatever it takes to bring them down.

Sister Grimm - Rachel Messina is the sixteen-year-old daughter of two of the world's oldest and most powerful dark magicians (who now pose as wealthy antique dealers). Before she runs away from home, the crafty raven-haired girl grabs a dusty tome filled with spells. Now calling herself "Sister Grimm," Rachel struggles to master these black magicks (despite her religious background). The other co-leader of the Runaways, Sister Grimm is romantically attached to Wilder.

Lucy in the Sky - Leslie Dean is a stunningly beautiful, happy-go-lucky, sixteen-year-old girl who never imagined that her parents were actually alien warlords (who hide from intergalactic police under the guise of earthly real estate magnates). In some ways, Leslie has it much harder than her fellow Runaways. Not only does she discover the awful truth about her parents, but she also learns that she's really an alien. Still, this revelation becomes a lot easier to accept when she finds that her otherworldly physiology allows her to fly. Taking her codename from a favorite song, "Lucy in the Sky" will discover new and wonderful powers every day she's on the team. If only she could get _____ to fall in love with her, her life would be complete.

Talkback - The team's only other male (tradition be damned!), John Stein is the sixteen-year-old son of two "mad scientists," a couple that claims to be nothing more than successful software engineers. Inheriting little of his parents' technical know-how (he would rather play lacrosse), John is nevertheless able to obtain experimental hi-tech gauntlets before escaping from his broken home. Dubbed "Talkback" by his teammates, John hates taking orders, preferring to fly headlong into battle. Thankfully, his extensive array of hi-tech gadgets usually prevents him from getting hurt. Talkback is more than a bit obsessed with Leslie, and he's constantly vying for her attention.

Arsenic & Old Lace - Ferociously independent (if a little socially inept), Gertie Yorkes isn't the least bit surprised to hear that her retired parents are actually time-traveling despots from an apocalyptic future. Eager to leave home, she takes something from her parents hidden sub-basement before jetting, a ferocious velociraptor genetically engineered in the 87th Century to telepathically serve its master (in this case, Gertie). Calling herself "Arsenic," Gertie names her loyal dinosaur "Old Lace." Together, they're an extremely formidable, extremely odd duo.

Bruiser - The youngest member of the Runaways, Molly Hayes is the thirteen-year-old homo superior daughter of two Hollywood actors (who are actually mutant terrorists). Shortly before joining the team, Molly discovers that her genetic makeup grants her extraordinary strength. The little girl can bench a city bus without breaking a sweat... but she'd much rather watch the new Kylie Minogue video on TRL. Gertie (who acts like an overprotective older sister around Molly), jokingly nicknames her "Bruiser," a handle that seems preposterous given her sweet and innocent exterior. Molly claims that she's eager to do the right thing, but deep down, she just misses her Mommy and Daddy.

THE TONE
I started getting into comics when I was about twelve, but I had almost no interest in books like Power Pack or Teen Titans. Even though they were well crafted, they seemed like they were aimed at little kids (which no twelve-year-olds think of themselves as). I was more interested in books like X-Men, cool stories about badass outcasts (which is what most twelve-year-olds think of themselves as).

Now that Grant Morrison is writing X-Men for readers my age, Marvel could use a new all-ages series that's smart and edgy, but also PG-rated and absolutely continuity-free. I'm confident The Runaways can be that book.

Combining action, romance, humor, and some Harry Potter-style darkness, The Runaways is a series that older readers will definitely enjoy, and a book that retailers can confidently put into the hands of younger customers (if such a thing still exists).

THE STORIES
Like the excellent first arc of Ultimate Spider-Man, we'll be starting from square one and taking time to tell a character-driven origin story. These are my tentative plans for our first six issues:

Issue #1 - We open with Spider-Man and Daredevil working together to capture the Hulk... only to reveal that this is actually teenager Alex Wilder playing an online role-playing game starring his favorite real-world superheroes. (This will quickly establish that our protagonist is a young, intelligent, contemporary aspiring hero.) Alex's parents barge in and order him off the computer. Their guests are about to arrive.

The Wilders are soon joined by five other wealthy families, each made up of two loving parents and their single child. As the grown-ups discuss their charity work in private, Alex is forced to entertain the other kids (which is almost as awkward as having to hang out with those strange second cousins you only see at Thanksgiving). Here, we quickly establish the basic relationships of the six teenagers: Alex and goth Rachel are attracted to each other, flighty Leslie has a secret crush on _____, jock John has a secret crush on Leslie, and everyone hates misfit Gertie, except for prepubescent Molly, who trusts the older girl enough to ask her about the "strange things" happening to her body.

Instead of playing Playstation like they normally do, the six teens decide to spy on their parents' private meeting. Watching from a secret passage Alex recently discovered, the kids are amazed to see the way the adults behave behind closed doors. But when Alex's father produces an orphaned infant (obtained on the black market) from inside a box, the suddenly troubled kids tell young Molly to shut her eyes. The teens watch in horror as their parents reveal their unique powers, and use them to perform some kind of dark sacrificial ritual.

After the baby is killed (off-panel!), the adults smile and toast, "To the end of the world as we know it." From their hidden vantage point behind a one-way mirror, the kids react with fear and disbelief. Suddenly, one of the adults turns to the mirror, and asks, "What was that noise?"

Issue #2 - The adults burst into the secret passageway... only to find it empty. They make sure that their children are still playing Playstation in another room, and return to their vile work. Alone again, the kids drop their calm facades and freak out. Did they really see what they thought they saw, or was it some kind of game? What the hell are they supposed to do now?

Rather than confront their apparently evil elders and possibly end up dead, the kids resolve to meet up in secret later that night (except for young Molly, who they decide to keep in the dark about this). They struggle to act natural when their parents finally exit their "meeting," and exchange terse farewells before leaving.

Escaping their homes after midnight, the kids reconvene at the parking lot of a nearby mall (minus young Molly). After much deliberation, they decide to call the Avengers and tell them about their parents' secret lives as super-villains. But when the Avengers' hotline is busy, they're forced to call a homicide detective at a local precinct. When the man laughs at their "evil parents" story, the kids realize that they're going to

have to find some hard evidence before anyone will believe them. Alex found nothing when he searched his home for the infant's corpse or any of the murder weapons used in the ritual, so the group decides to pile in John's van and check out Gertie's house next.

Sneaking inside (Gertie's parents are asleep), the kids soon find a secret passageway much like the one in Alex's house. Spelunking down a deep corridor, they suddenly hear something behind them. The kids turn to see a giant velociraptor baring its fangs!

Issue #3 - The group screams in terror, but the dinosaur politely bows in front of Gertie. A note around its neck explains that this beast was meant to be a gift for Gertie in the event of her time-traveling parents' death. The cyborg raptor responds only to her commands, and is trained to protect her from the countless enemies Gertie's evil mother and father have apparently made over the years. The kids scour the rest of the catacombs for evidence, but retreat after finding nothing (dinosaur in tow).

As relationships and jealousy blossom, the kids head to Rachel's home, where they eventually find a passageway in the woods behind her house. Inside, they discover the book of spells Rachel's warlock parents used during the sacrifice. But because of her Christian faith, Rachel refuses to try any of the "black spells" found inside. Desperate for more damning evidence, the group decides to press on.

Finally, the kids try the secret chamber inside Leslie's house (her parents are out of town), where the attractive young woman finds out about her alien heritage. At first, she's completely horrified, but when Leslie discovers that the "medical bracelet" she's been forced to wear her whole life is the only thing inhibiting her from using her power of flight, she perks right up. Unfortunately, the group finds nothing else of value, and so moves on to John's home.

Meanwhile, back at the police precinct the kids phoned last issue, the Captain asks one of his detectives about the strange call that came in earlier. The Captain laughs nervously when he hears the story about the kids and their "super-villain parents," but he soon retreats to his office and calls Alex's father, whispering, "My Lord, I think we may have a problem..."

Issue #4 - Inside a secret lab underneath John's house, the young athlete is shocked to learn that his parents appear to be brilliant mad scientists. How could a guy who flunked biology be the son of two scientific geniuses, the other kids wonder. John tries on a pair of hi-tech gauntlets, when he suddenly hears a voice say, "That's enough, children. I just received a troubling call from Alex's father. Your little scavenger hunt is over." The kids turn around to see John's parents, both wielding huge sci-fi weapons!

Gertie's pet raptor leaps to her defense, but is quickly neutralized. Alex leads the others in a decent fight, but they're no match for the two more experienced adults. The teenagers are almost defeated, when Rachel sacrifices her beliefs to cast a black spell that temporarily overpowers John's parents.

The kids are able to retreat, but Alex soon gets a call on his cell phone. It's his mother, who says, "Alex, you need to stop this immediately... or I'm afraid we'll have no choice but to do something terrible to your young friend Molly."

Issue #5 - Sick at the thought of anything happening to Molly, our heroes foolishly decide to rescue their youngest companion from the home of her evil mutant parents.

Naturally, when they arrive, the group is greeted by several adults, Rachel's mother, Gertie's father, and both of Molly's parents (who are using their perplexed daughter as a human shield). The teenagers use

what little they've learned about their weapons/abilities, but they're once again soundly defeated by their more powerful elders.

Molly's father is about to hurt her friend Gertie, when Molly suddenly breaks free of her mother's grasp and punches her father through a wall! Clearly, when Molly was telling Gertie about the changes happening to her body back in Issue #1, she didn't mean puberty... she meant the onset of her mutant powers!

This briefly turns the tide of the fight, and the kids barely escape alive. Before fleeing the house with Molly, Alex grabs something called "The Compendium," an encrypted book that appears to have information about the adults' clandestine organization, "The Pride."

Though they never found the body of the slain infant, the teenagers decide that they now have more than enough information to take to the authorities. But when one of the kids turns on the radio in John's van, they hear a startling report. The police are looking for a teenager named Alex Wilder... who apparently killed an infant in his own home. When interviewed, Alex's parents say that this murder "might have something to do with their son's involvement in violent online role-playing games," and the cops suspect that some of Alex's friends may have helped commit this heinous act.

Simultaneously, the framed kids say, "Oh, $#@*."

Issue #6 - Realizing that even the police are under the control of their parents' evil empire, our heroes are now wanted fugitives with no one to turn to. Rachel reveals that she has a secret hiding place that she's been going to since she was a little girl, and the group is forced to take shelter in this abandoned underground youth hospice.

Frightened and overwhelmed, the six formerly wealthy kids now have nothing but each other. Betrayed by their duplicitous families, the teenagers are united by their desire to do whatever it takes to destroy the Pride, and to right their parents' wrongs. Creating codenames and disguises for themselves, an unlikely new team of heroes is born.

Finally, in an intriguing epilogue to our first arc, we revisit the teenagers' assembled parents. The Pride is distraught by the evening's turn of events, but heartened by an unsigned electronic communiqué they receive. It reads, "Mom and Dad - I love you, and I know you have reasons for doing what you did. Don't worry, I will always be loyal to you."

The Next Arc - As the Runaways start to decode the Compendium they stole in our last storyline, they begin to realize just how powerful their parents really are, and how much damage their secret organization has done over the last twenty years. Accepting that they're not yet ready to take on the Pride, the masked teenagers decide to use their newfound powers to protect the community (and maybe atone for some of their parents' sins in the process). They start by attempting to capture a group of bank robbers terrorizing Los Angeles... but the Runaways soon discover that being a superhero isn't as easy as it looks on TV.

Meanwhile, romances and feuds between team members continue to develop. And elsewhere, the Pride comes up with an ambitious plan to lure their "wayward" children back home.

ADRIAN ALPHONA SKETCHBOOK

Nico — Karolina

Alex   Chase

PIXIE RANK

Molly

make her younger

Jacket

spiky
spiky
hair
piercings

Frills

Sister
Grimm

Alex

Gertie

blonde

real skinny...

LUCY
IN THE
SKY !!!

ARSENIC

funky hair?

BRUISER

PROMOTIONAL SKETCHES
BY ADRIAN ALPHONA

BRIAN K. VAUGHAN

The co-creator of *Runaways*, Brian K. Vaughan has written multiple Marvel miniseries, including *Chamber*, *Doctor Strange: The Oath*, *Hood* and *Spider-Man/Doctor Octopus: Negative Exposure*. Elsewhere, his best-known projects include *Y: The Last Man*, *Ex Machina* and the critically acclaimed graphic novel *Pride of Baghdad*. Born in Cleveland in 1976, Brian currently resides in California with his playwright wife, though he looks forward to leaving the evil home of the villainous Pride soon.

Brian pretended to run away when he was seven years old, though he really just hid behind a couch and waited patiently to hear how concerned his parents would be over his disappearance. Much to his disappointment, for at least the next twelve hours, his mom and dad went about their lives as if nothing were different. That was most likely the day that *Runaways* was born. (Brian's older brother swears that this story is completely imagined, but when has Brian ever lied?)

ADIAN ALPHONA

Canadian artist Adrian Alphona studied graphic design at Toronto's George Brown College and joined Toronto-based Bright Anvil Studios before he landed his first professional comic-book work as co-creator of *Runaways* with writer Brian K. Vaughan. While he designed all the early *Runaways* characters, Alphona has said he especially likes drawing Nico and Karolina. With writer G. Willow Wilson, he later launched the critically acclaimed All-New Marvel NOW! series *Ms. Marvel*.

DAVID NEWBOLD

In addition to Runaways, Kubert School graduate David Newbold has inked the one-shot *Weapon X: The Draft — Marrow*, and issues of *Deadpool*, *Marvel Age Fantastic Four* and *Marvel Age Spider-Man Team-Up*.

CRAIG YEUNG

Craig Yeung was born and raised in Toronto ON, Canada. After getting his Bachelor's degree, he went back to Ontario College of Art to pursue his love of comics and visual arts. His previous works include *Outlaw 7*, *Buffy the Vampire Slayer*, *Warhammer Monthly*, *Uncanny X-Men*, and *Marvel Age Spider-Man*. Craig currently works out of Bright Anvil Studios.

BRIAN REBER

Brian Reber has lent his impeccable sense of color to Marvel titles as *Runaways*, *X-Men: Legacy* and *X-Factor*. His credits also include *Batwing* and *Batman and the Outsiders* for DC Comics, and *X-O Manowar* and *Harbinger* for Valiant Entertainment.

CHRISTINA STRAIN

Once upon a time, there was a princess who colored for Crossgen. Two months later, Crossgen left her with a new and expensive lease on an apartment. Then she met a stable boy named Erik Ko who introduced her to two fairy godmothers — C.B. and MacKenzie. These two kind spirits granted Christina her wish to continue coloring and provided her with a brand new sparkly pair of magical shackles called *Runaways* and *Mary Jane* which led to her coloring many more Marvel titles, including *World War Hulk* and *S.H.I.E.L.D.*

JO CHEN

Born in Taipei, Taiwan on the 4th of July, Jo Chen began working in comics professionally at age 14, when Da Ran Publishing underwrote her comic group's first volume of short stories. Since immigrating to the U.S. with her family in 1994, she has continued to work steadily in the comic book industries in both hemispheres, publishing her double volume manga *The Other Side of the Mirror* in Asia, while establishing herself in the U.S. as a commodity with the majors.

In the intervening years, Jo has produced interiors and cover art for such series as Wildstorm's *Robotech* and *Racer X*, part of its successful *Speed Racer* series, Dreamwave's *Darkminds Macropolis*, D.C. Comics' *Robin* and *The Demon*, Vertigo's *Fight For Tomorrow*, UDON's *Street Fighter*, Top Cow's *Battle of the Planets*, Marvel's *Taskmaster*, *Thor: Son of Asgard* and *Runaways*, and has most recently collaborated with Joss Whedon, the creator of *Buffy the Vampire Slayer*, and Dark Horse Comics on work for *Serenity*, as a tie-in with the release of the motion picture. She is now hard at work with writer Brian K. Vaughan and editor MacKenzie Cadenhead on the final covers for the *Runaways* second series. When Jo has a few moments to spare, she works on interiors for her doujin *Cruel to be Kind* and fleshes out character designs for her Chinese-mythological saga *The Specter King*.

TAKESHI MIYAZAWA

Canadian artist Takeshi Miyazawa developed his style from his lifelong love of anime and manga. His unique artistry first flavored projects including *Sidekicks*, *Runaways* and *Amazing Fantasy*, leading to his crowning achievement at *Marvel: Spider-Man Loves Mary Jane* in collaboration with writer Sean McKeever. Other projects include a return engagement with *Runaways* and *Secret Invasion: Runaways/Young Avengers*.